CONTENTS

ARRIVALS

Unit 1

A: Excuse me. Dolores Cotten?
B: Yes?
A: Hi. I'm Brad Jordan, from Orange Computers. How do you do?
B: How do you do? I'm glad to meet you, Brad. Thank you for coming to meet us.
A: It's a pleasure. How was the trip?
B: It was fine, thanks. Oh, I'd like you to meet Ron Eng. He's our sales manager.
A: How do you do, Ron?

Exercise 1
A: Bob Crawford?
B: . . .
A: Hello. I'm Helen Kirby, from General Technologies. How do you do?
B: . . .
A: It's a pleasure. Did you have a good trip?
B: . . .
A: Oh, let me introduce you to Charlie Vitto. He's our financial manager.
B: . . .

C: Karen!
D: Hi, Jody. How are you doing?
C: Just fine. How are you? I haven't seen you for ages.
D: I'm all right. Are you here to meet somebody?
C: No, my mother just left for Miami.
D: Do you have time for coffee?
C: Sure. I'd love a cup.

E: Margaret, hi.
F: Hello, Carol. How are you?
E: Oh, I'm O.K. How are you getting along?
F: Fine, thanks. How are Larry and the kids?
E: Everybody's fine. My car's just outside. Let me take one of your bags.
F: Oh, thanks. Careful, it's heavy.

G: Hi. What time is your next flight to New York?
H: 2:45. Flight 604 to Kennedy Airport. There is space available.
G: What's the fare—one way?
H: It's $56.70 with the tax.
G: O.K. Here you are. Put it on my Diners Club card, please.
H: All right. Just a second.

Exercise 2
Look at the conversation between G and H, and practice two similar conversations, one for New York and one for Chicago.

Streamline Air Departures from Middleburg		
Service to	Flight	Departs
New York (La Guardia)	317	11:05
New York (JFK)	604	2:45
Los Angeles	410	4:15
Chicago (O'Hare)	104	3:55
Atlanta	211	10:20

Streamline Air Fares (tax included)			
From Middleburg	Mon–Thurs	Week-ends	*Super Saver
To New York one way	$56.70	$76.70	$89.00
round trip	$113.40	$153.40	—
To Chicago one way	$47.30	$65.30	$79.00
round trip	$94.60	$130.60	—

* Make reservation & buy ticket 2 weeks ahead.

I: Well, hi there!
J: Uh—hello.
I: How are you doing?
J: Oh—fine. Uh—excuse me . . . do I know you from somewhere?
I: Sure, it's me, Rick Ballestrina.
J: I'm sorry. I don't think I know you.
I: Aren't you Jose Cortes?
J: No, I'm afraid not.
I: Oh, forgive me. I thought you were someone else. I'm so sorry.
J: That's all right.

Exercise 3
Listen to the airport announcements. Look at the example and complete the chart in the same way.

Airline	Flight	To	Gate	Departs
1. Streamline	604	New York (JFK)	3	2:45
2.				
3.				
4.				
5.				

Exercise 4
How are you?
I'm fine, thanks. How are you?
1. Hi!
2. I'm so sorry.
3. Thank you very much for helping me.
4. Aren't you Michael Jackson?
5. How are you getting along?
6. Here you are.
7. Excuse me.
8. Good-bye.

Unit 1

IS EVERYTHING READY?

RALPH & EDWARD PRODUCTIONS

Program: This Is Your Life
Date: Nov. 3
Origin: KRKR, Los Angeles
Studio: 4
Subject: William Paine
Host: Joe Campanaro
Director: Chris Price

Running order

Pre-show
7:00 Admit studio audience.
7:30 Warm up (Comedian tells jokes to audience).
7:55 Limousine arrives (7-minute walk to studio).

Show
8:00 Start titles, music, commercial (Fizz).
8:01 Campanaro introduces show.
8:02 Paine arrives. Campanaro greets him.

Guests
8:03 Paine's sister from Japan.
8:05 His schoolteacher.
8:08 Commercials (Dr. Peppy & Daft Cheese).
8:09 Rita Colon, actress.
8:11 Mother.
8:12 Father.
8:14 John Galveston, movie director.
8:16 Commercials (Fizz & Daft Mayonnaise).
8:18 His first girlfriend.
8:19 Steve Newman, actor (his best friend).
8:21 Donna Parrot, Hollywood reporter.
8:23 Clips from Paine's latest movie.
8:27 His brother.
8:28 Commercials (Dr. Peppy & Alarmin Tissue).
8:29 Show ends. Start credits and music.

Post-show
8:30-8:45 Studio audience leaves.
8:45 Champagne party for Paine and guests.

"This Is Your Life" used to be one of the most popular programs on American television. Recently one of the national networks started the program again—not reruns but all-new shows. Every week a well-known person is invited to a TV studio, without knowing that he or she will be the subject of the program. The host greets the person with "This Is Your Life!" The person then meets friends and relatives from his or her past and present. The program is taped before a live audience. The taping begins at 8:00. It's 6:45 now and the director is checking the preparations with her new production assistant. The subject of tonight's show will be an actor, William Paine. The host, as usual, will be Joe Campanaro.

Director: Let's check the arrangements. We're bringing Bill Paine here in a rented limousine. He thinks he's coming to tape a talk show appearance. The driver has been told to arrive at exactly 7:55. The program begins at 8:00. At that time Bill will be walking to the studio. Joe will start his introduction at 8:01, and Bill will get here at 8:02. Joe will meet him at the door. Camera 4 will be there. Then he'll take him to that sofa. It'll be on Camera 3. Bill will be sitting there during the whole program. For most of the show Joe will be sitting next to the sofa or standing on that "X." He'll be on Camera 2. The guests will come through that door, talk to Bill and Joe, and then go backstage.

Director: Now, is that clear?
Production Assistant: Yes, but—uh—there is one thing.
Director: Well, what is it?
PA: Who's going to take care of the guests before they come on?
Director: Stephanie is.
PA: And where will they be waiting?
Director: In Room 401 we have a guest lounge. Stephanie will be sitting there with them. They'll be watching the show on a monitor. She'll cue them two minutes before they come on.
PA: O.K. I think that covers everything.

Exercise 1
Each of the guests will say a few words about William Paine.
A: *Who'll be speaking at 8:06?*
B: *His school teacher will.*
Ask and answer about: 8:04, 8:10, 8:15, 8:19, and 8:27.

Exercise 2
A: *What'll be happening at 7:45?*
B: *A comedian will be telling jokes to the audience.*
Ask and answer about: 7:57, 8:35, and 9:00.

Exercise 3
The guests will be waiting in Room 401 from 7:50 until they go on.
A: *How long will his sister be waiting?*
B: *She'll be waiting for thirteen minutes.*
Ask and answer about the other guests.

American STREAMLINE

BERNARD HARTLEY & PETER VINEY
DESTINATIONS
PART A: UNITS 1–40

An intensive American English course
for advanced students
Student's Edition

American adaptation by Flamm/Northam Authors and Publishers Services, Inc.

Oxford University Press

Oxford University Press
200 Madison Avenue New York, N.Y. 10016 USA
Walton Street Oxford OX2 6DP England
OXFORD is a trademark of Oxford University Press.
© B. Hartley, P. Viney,
and Oxford University Press, 1985
First published 1985
Printing (last digit): 10 9 8 7

Library of Congress Cataloging in Publication Data

Hartley, Bernard
American Streamline Destinations

"American adaptation by Flamm/Northam Authors
and Publishers Services, Inc."

ISBN 0-19-434184-4 (Student's ed. Part A)
ISBN 0-19-434185-2 (Student's ed. Part B)
ISBN 0-19-434120-8 (complete student's ed.)
ISBN 0-19-434121-6 (teacher's ed.)
ISBN 0-19-434124-0 (cassette)

Illustrations by:
Cover: Paul Thomas; Unit 2: Hilary Newby/Publishers Graphics; Unit 3: Paddy Mounter; Unit 4: London Art Technical Drawings, Ltd.; Unit 10: Llynne Buschman; Unit 11: Bonnie Dann; Units 12 and 13: Irene Trivas/Publishers Graphics; Unit 20: Ken Cox; Unit 21: Paul Sample; Unit 22: Bonnie Dann; Unit 23: Susanna Ray; Unit 25: Hilary Newby/Publishers Graphics; Units 28 and 29: Richard Draper; Units 31 and 34: Paddy Mounter; Unit 36: Ellis Nadler; Unit 37: Irene Trivas/Publishers Graphics; Unit 38: Bonnie Dann; Unit 39: Ken Cox; Unit 44: Llynne Buschman; Unit 45: Mike Vaughan; Unit 46: Richard Draper; Unit 47: Bill Prosser; Unit 53: Llynne Buschman; Unit 62: Bonnie Dann; Unit 63: Paul Sample; Unit 65: Mike Saunders; Unit 66: Ron Jobson; Unit 67: Paddy Mounter; Units 68 and 71: Llynne Buschman; Unit 72: Paul Sample; Unit 73: Leslie Dunlap/Publishers Graphics; Unit 74: Llynne Buschman; Unit 80: Paul Sample.

Photographs by:
Units 1, 18, 27, 52 (man and baby), 59 (cab drivers): Catherine Noren; Units 14, 15, 33 (collage), 41, 48 (bottom), 60 and 77 (background): Halley Ganges. Unit 4: courtesy of Fiat; Unit 7: C. Vergara/Photo Researchers; Unit 9: Camera Press; Unit 16: John Topham Picture Library; Unit 19: P and PF James; Unit 32: UPI/Bettmann; Unit 33: published with permission of The Dallas Morning News; Copyright © 1980 by The New York Times Company. Reprinted by permission; Reprinted with permission of the Village Voice © 1980; Reprinted by permission of New York News Inc. © 1980 New York News Inc. © News Group Chicago, Inc., 1980 Reprinted with permission of the Chicago Sun-Times; Reprinted by permission of the San Francisco Examiner; Reprinted by permission of the Miami Herald; Unit 40: left-hand page: (cable car) Image Bank; (Las Vegas and Grand Canyon and Minnie Mouse) Alan Hutchinson; right-hand page: (background and bottom left) Image Bank; (top left and middle) Colorific; Unit 41: Reprint by permission of Nissin Foods(USA)Co.,Inc.; Unit 42: Terry Williams; Unit 48: (top) Keyston Press Agency Ltd.; Unit 51: (top) Metropolitan Home Magazine © Meredith Corporation 1984. All rights reserved; (bottom) Elizabeth Whiting and Associates; Unit 52: (Debra Harry, Telly Savalas) Syndication International; (Lauren Bacall) Rex Features; Unit 56: Sunday Times; Unit 57: The Kobal Collection; Unit 59: (bottom) Karen Wollman; Unit 66: (satellite) Elizabeth Photo Library; (Saturn) Sunday Times/NASA; (plaque and earth) Space Frontiers; Unit 69: Tom McHugh/Photo Researchers; Unit 70: BBC Hulton Picture Library; Western Americana Picture Library; Unit 78: Jean Photographs.

The publishers would also like to thank the following for their time and assistance:

All-City Appliance   Gordon Fraser Gallery
Bell & Howell   Hallmark Cards, Inc.
Eastern Airlines   McDonald's Corporation
Goodyear Tire and
    Rubber Company

Printed in Hong Kong

THIS IS YOUR LIFE!

Campanaro: Good evening and welcome to "This Is Your Life." I'm your host, Joe Campanaro. We're waiting for the subject of tonight's program. He's one of the world's leading actors, and he thinks he's coming here for a talk show. I think I hear him now ... Yes, here he is! William Paine, this is your life!

Paine: Oh, no! I can't believe it! Not me ...

Campanaro: Yes, you! Come in with me now. Ladies and gentlemen, William Paine! (Applause.) Sit right over here, Bill. Let's begin at the beginning. You were born in Providence, Rhode Island on July 2, 1942. You were the youngest of six children. Your mother was a model, and your father worked at a furniture store. Of course, your name was Herman Wartski then.

Campanaro: Do you recognize this voice?
Voice: I remember Herm—Bill—when he was two. He used to cry and scream all day.
Paine: Rosanne!
Campanaro: Yes, all the way from Tokyo—we flew her here to be with you tonight—your sister, Rosanne Wartski Tatsukawa.
Paine: Rosie, why didn't you tell me?
Campanaro: Yes, you haven't seen each other for 9 years. Take a seat next to him, Rosanne. You went to school in Providence and got your diploma from Whitney High School in 1960.

Campanaro: Do you remember this voice?
Voice: Herman! Stop daydreaming! I asked you a question!
Paine: Incredible! It's Mr. Theissen.
Campanaro: Your English teacher, Mr. Irwin Theissen. Was Bill a good student, Mr. Theissen?
Theissen: Well, not really. No, he was the worst in the class. But he was a great actor, even in those days. He could imitate all the teachers.
Campanaro: Thank you, Mr. Theissen. You can talk to Bill later. Well, you went on to the Yale School of Drama in 1962 and finished in 1966. In 1970 you went to Hollywood.

Campanaro: Do you know this voice?
Voice: Say, Bill, can you ride a horse yet?
Paine: Rita!
Campanaro: Yes, Rita Colon, who's flown in from New York, where she's appearing in the musical *34th Street.*
Colon: Bill, darling! It's so wonderful to see you. Hello, Joe, darling. Bill and I were in a movie together in 1974. Bill had to learn to ride a horse, and ... well, Bill doesn't like horses very much.
Paine: Like them? I'm scared to death of them!
Colon: Anyway, poor Bill practiced for 2 weeks. Then he went to the

director—it was John Galveston—and said, "What do you want me to do?" John said, "I want you to fall off the horse." Bill was furious. He said, "What?! Fall off?! I've been practicing for two weeks. I could fall off the first day—without any practice!"

Look at this:

Ralph & Edward Productions	
Program:	*This Is Your Life*
Date:	*Nov. 3*
Origin:	*KRKR, Los Angeles*
Studio:	*4*
Subject:	*William Paine*
Host:	*Joe Campanaro*
Director:	*Chris Price*

Subject's Biographical Data

Last name:	*Wartski (stage name)*
First name:	*Herman (William Paine)*
Middle name/initial:	*I.*
Date of birth:	*7/2/42*
Place of birth:	*Providence, R.I.*
Nationality:	*American (U.S.)*
Education:	*Whitney H.S. Providence Yale School of Drama*
Address:	*77 Sunshine Boulevard Hollywood, CA.*
Marital status:	*Single*
Occupation:	*Actor*

Ralph & Edward Productions	
Program:	
Date:	
Origin:	
Studio:	
Subject:	
Host:	
Director:	

Subject's Biographical Data

Last name:	
First name:	
Middle name/initial:	
Date of birth:	
Place of birth:	
Nationality:	
Education:	
Address:	
Marital status:	
Occupation:	

Ask questions and fill out the form for another student.

HELSINKI
STOCKHOLM
1 278km
2 657km
COPENHAGEN
GLASGOW
1 475km
YORK
3 798km
2 730km
DOVER
FRANKFURT
4 631km
3 640km
GENEVA
4 438km
4 632km
BELGRADE
3 648km
CLERMONT-FERRAND
5 521km
CORUNA
4 753km
TRIESTE
BARCELONA
1 623km
2 724km
MONTE CARLO
LISBON
3 705km
MADRID

Driver: Russell Cook
Nationality: British *Age:* 28
Starting point: Glasgow
Car: Talbot Sunbeam Lotus
Engine displacement: 132 cu. in
  (2172cc)
Top speed: 122 mph
Fuel economy: city 18 mpg, highway
  22 mpg
Overall dimensions
  Length: 150.4 in (382 cm)
  Width: 63 in (160 cm)
  Height: 54.7 in (139 cm)

Driver: Hannu Larsen
Nationality: Finnish *Age:* 32
Starting point: Helsinki
Car: Audi Quattro
Engine displacement: 131 cu. in (2144
  cc)
Top speed: 137 mph
Fuel economy: city 18 mpg, highway
  35 mpg
Overall dimensions
  Length: 173 in (440 cm)
  Width: 67.7 in (172 cm)
  Height: 52.8 in (134 cm)

Driver: Danielle Bernard
Nationality: French *Age:* 31
Starting point: Lisbon
Car: Renault 5 Gordini
Engine displacement: 85.2 cu. in
  (1397cc)
Top speed: 115 mph
Fuel economy: city 31 mpg, highway
  45 mpg
Overall dimensions
  Length: 137.8 in (350 cm)
  Width: 59.8 in (152 cm)
  Height: 54.7 in (139 cm)

Start

Sunday

Monday

Tuesday

Wednesday

Thursday

2 703km

THESSALONIKI

1 543km

ATHENS

Driver: Sandro Rossi
Nationality: Italian   *Age:* 30
Starting point: Athens
Car: Fiat 131
Engine displacement: 97 cu. in
   (1585cc)
Top speed: 104 mph
Fuel economy: city 27 mpg, highway
   38 mpg
Overall dimensions
   Length: 167.7 in (426 cm)
   Width: 65 in (165 cm)
   Height: 54.7 in (139 cm)

THE
MONTE CARLO RALLY

The Monte Carlo Rally, which started in 1911, is Europe's most famous car event. Competitors leave from several points around Europe and follow routes of approximately equal length to a rallying point which will be Geneva this year. Then they follow a single route to the finish. The rally consists of five daily stages, beginning on Sunday morning, and each competitor will have driven about 2000 miles by Thursday night. It is not a race. The winner is decided on a points system. Drivers have to maintain an average speed between control points, and there are also special tests of driving skill in different conditions on the way.

Rally News from CSN, Cable Sports Network

Now here's a report from Howard Sokell in England.

Hello from Dover. It's 9 o'clock on Monday, January 25th, and the British competitors in the Monte Carlo Rally have just arrived here at the end of the second stage in this year's contest. Russell Cook, who's driving a Sunbeam Lotus, is in the lead. The Triumph, driven by Tony Bond, who won last year's rally, crashed in Yorkshire this morning. Tony was not hurt, but he will be unable to continue. Seven other cars have withdrawn due to bad weather conditions. Tonight the cars, which left from Glasgow on Sunday morning, will be crossing the English Channel.

Exercise 1
Look at the first driver.
What's his name?
His name's Russell Cook.
Where does he come from?
He comes from Britain.
How old is he? He's 28.
Ask and answer questions about the other drivers.

Exercise 2
Look at the first car. (All statistics are for production cars.)
What make is it? It's a Sunbeam Lotus.

How fast can it go? The top speed is 122 mph.
How much gas does it use? 18 mpg in the city, 22 mpg on the highway.
How long is it? 150.4 in.
How wide is it? 63 in.
How high is it? It's 54.7 in.
Ask and answer questions about the other cars.

Exercise 3
Look at the drivers and the cars.
Danielle Bernard's older than Sandro Rossi.
Russell Cook isn't as old as Danielle Bernard.
Hannu Larsen's the oldest.
Make comparisons about the cars using: fast/long/wide/high/economical.

Exercise 4
Look at the first driver. All the cars started on Sunday morning.
Where is he now? He's in Dover.
Where did he start? He started in Glasgow.
How long has he been driving? He's been driving for two days.
How many miles has he driven? 748 miles.
Ask and answer questions about the other drivers.

Exercise 5
Look at the first driver. It's Monday night.
Where will he be tomorrow night?
He'll be in Clermont-Ferrand.
What will he be doing tomorrow?
He'll be driving from Dover to Clermont-Ferrand.
Ask and answer questions about Wednesday and Thursday.
Do the same for the other drivers.

Exercise 6
Look at the first driver.
On Tuesday night he'll be in Clermont-Ferrand.
How far will he have driven on Tuesday? He'll have driven 397 miles.
Ask and answer questions about Wednesday and Thursday.
Do the same for the other drivers.

OUT OF WORK

In the United States a lot of people are out of work. Tracy Kowalski is 19. She dropped out of high school two years ago and got a job as a check-out clerk in a supermarket. She was fired four months ago and hasn't been able to find another job yet.

"My old man just doesn't understand. He started working in the steel mill here in town when he was 16. Things are different now, but he thinks I should start bringing home some money. I'm on unemployment, but it isn't very much and I'm just fed up with standing in line to sign for it every other week. I hate having to ask my folks for money. My mom gives me a couple of dollars now and then, but she can't stand having me around the house all day. I've almost given up looking for a job. I look at the paper every day, but I'm really tired of going through the want ads. There are at least fifty people for every job. I was interested in becoming a receptionist for a dentist or a doctor because I like meeting people, but now I'd take any job that came along. People ask me why I don't move to California or maybe Houston, but I really don't want to leave my family and my friends. Anyway, I'd be scared of living all alone in a strange place."

Tracy went to the state employment office. She had to fill out a questionnaire. Here is part of it:

QUESTIONNAIRE

1. Do you want (check one)
   (a) full-time employment ☐
   (b) part-time employment ☐
2. What is most important for you?
   (Number these from 1 to 5 in order of importance — 1 = most, 5 = least)
   (a) money ☐ (b) people ☐
   (c) job security ☐ (d) job satisfaction ☐
   (e) interesting job ☐
3. Do you like (check "yes" or "no")

	yes	no
(a) meeting people?	☐	☐
(b) working alone?	☐	☐
(c) working with other people?	☐	☐
(d) working with your hands?	☐	☐
(e) traveling?	☐	☐
(f) working outdoors?	☐	☐

4. What do you do in your free time?
   (check "often", "sometimes", or "never")

George Hartman is 54. Until last year he was a foreman at an automobile plant in Michigan. He had worked for the same company since he graduated from high school. He had a good job and a comfortable life. When the company cut back production last year, George was laid off.

"It's funny, you know. I don't feel old, but it isn't easy to start looking for a job at my age. I've been turned down so many times that now I'm afraid of applying for a job. All the interviewers are twenty years younger than me. You see, I'm interested in learning a new skill, but nobody wants to train me. I can see their point of view, you know. I'll have to retire in a few years. It's just that . . . well, I'm tired of sitting around the house. I've worked hard for over thirty-five years, and now I'm terrified of having nothing to do. When I was still with U.S. Motors I was bored with doing the same thing day after day, but now I'd enjoy having a job again—any job. It's not just the money. I'm still on unemployment, and my wife has a good job. She makes more money than I ever did, but we have to be careful with expenses, and so I've given up smoking. But we're getting along. No, it's not just the money. I need to get out more and feel . . . useful, you know. Yeah, I guess I want to feel useful."

Exercise 1
I like meeting people.
Make sentences about yourself with: love/enjoy/like/don't like/dislike/hate/can't stand.

Exercise 2
I'm scared of living all alone.
Make sentences about yourself with: afraid of/terrified of/scared of.

Exercise 3
I'm bored with doing the same things.
Make sentences about yourself with: fed up with/bored with/tired of/interested in.

Exercise 4
I gave up smoking.
Make sentences about yourself with: start/begin/stop/give up.

GETTING A JOB

In the United States every state has an employment service which helps unemployed people who are looking for jobs. The local offices list job openings in the area, and give practical advice on interview techniques, application forms, letters, unemployment insurance, and Social Security. Young people, especially those without a college education, need to have this advice. Here is part of a brochure put out by one state.

THE INTERVIEW

So you're going to have an interview for a job. Great! Now for the hard part. To do well on an interview you need to give it some thought first. Employers want to learn if you are the person they want, so you'll be asked a lot about yourself. Think about it now, and you'll be able to give clear answers:

What do I do well?   School activities?
What are my good points?   School subjects?
Why would I like this job?   Previous job?
Spare-time interests?   Part-time work?
What is my family like?

What do I like doing and why?
What do I not like doing and why?

You will want to ask questions too:
The job itself?   Can I see
Training?   where I
Prospects for advancement?   would be
Educational opportunities?   working?
Conditions?   Hours?
                                   $ $ $?

Write down your answers and go over them just before you go into the interview.

BEFORE THE INTERVIEW

1. Find out all you can about the company.
2. Find out the interviewer's name and office phone number.
3. Find out where the interview is.
4. Find out how to get there and how long it will take you to get there.
5. Make sure you know what the job involves.
6. Dress to look clean and neat.

AT THE INTERVIEW

DOs
1. Arrive early. Call ahead if you're delayed.
2. Try to smile and show confidence.
3. Ask questions and show interest in the job.
4. Be polite, listen carefully, and speak clearly.
DON'Ts
1. Don't panic, even if faced by more than one person. (Breathe deeply and remember all your good points.)
2. Don't slouch or look bored. (Stand and sit straight; make eye contact.)
3. Don't smoke or chew gum.
4. Don't give one-word answers or say you don't care what you do.

Look at these ads for job openings.

Computer Operator
Experienced assistant IBM System 34. Duties: billing and inventory. Send resume or letter stating qualifications to: American Diversified, 485 5th Avenue, Beaver Falls, PA 15010.
Equal Opportunity Employer M/F

Dental Receptionist/Secretary
Part-time. Bilingual Spanish/English. Mature, bright. Respond with qualifications and salary requirements. Larkin Agency, 254 23rd Street, Pittsburgh, PA 15260.

Matsuda of Tokyo
Opportunities available for salesperson in Philadelphia boutique. Send resume with salary requirement and references to Nicole, 109 Broad St., Philadelphia, PA 19105.

A letter of application

1. Remember that the first impression is very important.
2. Type the letter neatly on good stationery.
3. Check for spelling mistakes. Use a dictionary if you are not sure of a word. Retype the letter if necessary.
4. Describe yourself, your qualifications, and your experience clearly.
5. If the ad tells you to write for an application form you do not need to give detailed information in your letter.
6. Follow standard business letter format. Address the letter and envelope clearly.

421 Lafayette Drive, Apt. 317
St. Paul, Minnesota 55105
April 4, 1984

Personnel Department
Continental Computer Corp.
935 Watson Ave.
St. Paul, MN 55101

Dear Sir or Madam:

In reference to your ad in today's *Standard*, I am interested in the opening for a trainee computer programmer. Please send me an application form and any further details. Thank you for your attention in this matter.

Yours truly,

Ashley Wychulis

Ashley Wychulis

BATTLE OF SHERIDAN STREET

By MARVIN ROTHSTEIN

Police and Housing Authority officials had to turn back again yesterday when they tried to talk to Mrs. Florence Hamilton. They estimated that at least twenty of Mrs. Hamilton's dogs (the exact number of dogs living with Mrs. Hamilton is not known) guarded both the front and back doors of her house at 875 Sheridan Street in the city's East Side section.

The city officials were hoping to speak to the 83-year old widow, who is still refusing to leave her home. Every other house in an area of several city blocks around Mrs. Hamilton's house has been demolished.

The Housing Authority plans to build a low-income housing project in the area. All of the other residents agreed to move when the Authority offered to relocate them to new apartments in the Hillside section.

Police wanted to use stronger methods to remove Mrs. Hamilton and her dogs from their house, but public opinion has forced them to take a more cautious approach.

continued on page B3

Channel 7 Newsdesk

Remember the lady and her dogs on Sheridan Street? We promised to follow the story, and tonight we have two reports. First, Alan Nelson at City Hall.

Report 1

Alan: The City Housing Authority isn't working on anything except the "Battle of Sheridan Street." It's one lady and her pets versus City Hall, and so far she's winning. I have here Ms. Hilda Martinez, the Director of the Housing Authority who has agreed to talk to us. Ms. Martinez, has the situation changed since yesterday?

Martinez: No, Alan, it hasn't. Mrs. Hamilton is still in her house, and she still refuses to talk to us.

Alan: What are you going to do?

Martinez: It's a touchy situation. We'd like her to come out peacefully. The police don't intend to arrest her, but she's a very stubborn lady!

Alan: Stubborn? Well, it is her home.

Martinez: Yes, and it's been her home for a long time, I know. But nobody else refused to move. You see, we're going to build 400 apartments in that area. We expect to have about 1200 people living there when the project is finished. You have to balance that against one person and a pack of dogs.

Alan: But Mrs. Hamilton was born in that house, and she tries to give a home to the poor homeless dogs of this city.

Martinez: Of course. But we have promised to relocate her and one of her dogs to a modern apartment in a senior citizens project. The other dogs will go to the ASPCA.

Alan: So, what happens next?

Martinez: We can't wait forever. We want the ASPCA to take all the dogs first. Then we hope to talk to Mrs. Hamilton and convince her to move. We have to do something soon.

Alan: This has been Alan Nelson for Channel 7 Newsdesk.

Report 2

Cindy Wong: I'm standing in front of the only house still occupied on the 800 block of Sheridan Street. We have managed to set up an interview with Mrs. Florence Hamilton, the occupant of the house. She has decided to speak to us, but she has demanded to see me alone except for a camera crew of two.

Cindy: Mrs. Hamilton, our viewers would like to hear your side of the story.

Hamilton: There's not much to say. They want me to move. I was born here, and I intend to die here. It's as simple as that. Down, Caesar! Sit! Cleo! Sit!

Cindy: But the Housing Authority really needs to have this land, and they have arranged to relocate you.

Hamilton: I know. But I can't take all my dogs, just one. I love them all, and I need to have company. They're all I have. Come back, Calpurnia! Sit! Sit!

Cindy: How long can you hold out here?

Hamilton: Oh, I have plenty of food. People bring me dog food. The city has threatened to cut off my water and lights, but I'll be all right.

Cindy: Thank you, Mrs. Hamilton.

Hamilton: You can tell the city for me that I want a house where I can keep my dogs, not a *(bleep)* apartment for *(bleep)* senior citizens!

Cindy: Uh, yes—uh, this has been Cindy Wong talking to Mrs. Florence Hamilton, who is fighting to keep her home and pets, for Channel 7 Newsdesk.

Exercise

" . . . the other residents **agreed to move** . . ." *Agreed to move* is verb + *to* + verb.

Read the page again and pick out the other examples of verbs with *to* and another verb.

SENDING A CARD

Greeting cards are big business in the United States. Millions of cards are sent every year, and you can buy cards for every special occasion—or for no particular occasion at all. You can send cards for Christmas, New Year's, Easter, birthdays, engagements, weddings, funerals, Valentine's Day, Mother's Day, Father's Day, Thanksgiving, Halloween, sickness, graduation, promotion, or just friendship.

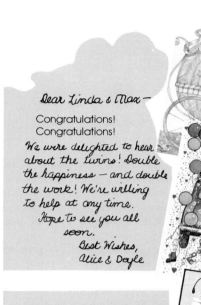

Dear Linda & Max —

Congratulations! Congratulations!

We were delighted to hear about the twins! Double the happiness — and double the work! We're willing to help at any time. Hope to see you all soon.

Best Wishes, Alice & Doyle

Sandy,

You now hold the key to the world!

Happy Sweet Sixteen!

Now my girl's Sweet Sixteen — a magical birthday. It's great to be young and have your whole life ahead of you.

Love, Uncle Dave

Dear Patsy:

Best Wishes on your Wedding.

I was so happy to hear about your engagement. I'm sorry to miss the happy event. I wish I could be there. I'm anxious to hear all the details of your wedding and honeymoon.

All the best, Deb

Dixie Lee & Beau,

Congratulations on your Silver Wedding Anniversary

Twenty-five years together! Neither of you look old enough to have a 25th anniversary. We're so happy for you and feel so lucky to have you as neighbors.

Gloria & Julio

With Sincere Sympathy

Jim—

I was so sorry to hear about your dad's passing. It's difficult to put into words how much he meant to me. I remember when he was our Little League coach. He was always ready to help me develop my abilities. I'm sorry I was unable to come to the funeral. Please express my condolences to your family.

Reggie

Dear Martha,

Get Well Soon

I was very upset to hear about your accident. I'll come to see you as soon as you can have visitors. I've enclosed something funny to read to keep your spirits up. I hope you get better soon.

Love, Rachel

Wedding anniversaries

The traditional gifts for each anniversary:

1st	paper	25th	silver
2nd	cotton	30th	pearl
3rd	leather	35th	jade
4th	linen	40th	ruby
5th	wood	45th	sapphire
10th	tin	50th	gold
15th	crystal	55th	emerald
20th	china	60th	diamond

Exercise

Can you suggest a suitable gift for each anniversary?
2nd anniversary
You could give a table cloth or some towels.

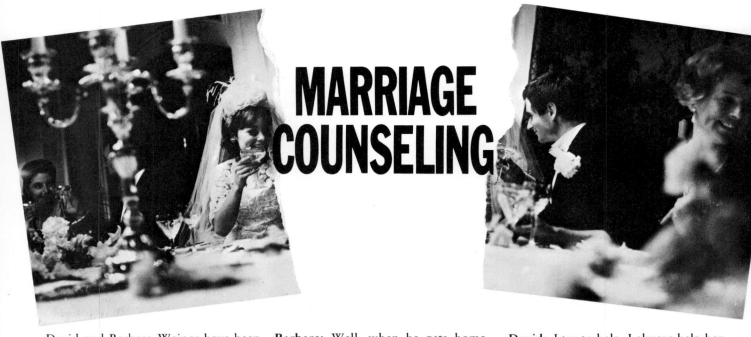

MARRIAGE COUNSELING

David and Barbara Weiner have been married for nearly fifteen years. They have two children, Gary, aged eleven, and Debbie, who is nine. During the last couple of years David and Barbara haven't been very happy. They argue all the time. Barbara's sister advised them to go to a marriage counselor. A marriage counselor helps married couples to talk about their problems and to solve them, if possible. Sometimes they meet the counselor separately, and other times they are together for the session. This is David and Barbara's third session with Dr. Joyce Sisters, the counselor.

Barbara's Interview

Dr. Sisters: Oh, come in, Barbara. Have a seat. Didn't David come?

Barbara: Yes, he's waiting outside. He didn't want to come here this week, but . . . well, I persuaded him to come.

Dr. Sisters: I see. How have things been going?

Barbara: Oh, about the same. We still seem to have fights all the time.

Dr. Sisters: What do you fight about?

Barbara: What don't we fight about? Oh, everything. You see, he's so inconsiderate . . .

Dr. Sisters: Go on.

Barbara: Well, I'll give you an example. You know, when the children started school, I wanted to go back to work again. So I got a job. Well, anyway, by the time I've picked Gary and Debbie up at school, I only get home about half an hour before David.

Dr. Sisters: Yes?

Barbara: Well, when he gets home, he expects me to run around and get dinner on the table. He never does anything in the house.

Dr. Sisters: Hmm.

Barbara: And last Friday! He invited three of his friends to come over for a drink. He didn't tell me to expect them, and I'd had a long hard day. I don't think that's right, do you?

Dr. Sisters: Barbara, I'm not here to pass judgement. I'm here to listen.

Barbara: I'm sorry. And he's so messy. He's worse than the kids. I always have to remind him to pick up his clothes. He just throws them on the floor. After all, I'm not his maid. I have my own career. Actually, I think that's part of the trouble. You see, I make more money than he does.

David's Interview

Dr. Sisters: David! I'm so glad you could come.

David: Hello, Dr. Sisters. Well, I'll be honest. Barbara had to force me to come, really.

Dr. Sisters: Does it embarrass you to talk about your problems?

David: Sure, it does. But I guess we need to talk to somebody.

Dr. Sisters: Barbara feels that you . . . well, that you resent her job.

David: I don't know. I'd like her to stay home, but she's very smart. So really, I encouraged her to go back to work. With the kids in school, she needs something to do. And I suppose we need the money.

Dr. Sisters: How do you share the housework?

David: I try to help. I always help her with the dishes, and I help Gary and Debbie to do their homework while she makes dinner. But she doesn't think that's enough. What do you think?

Dr. Sisters: I'm not here to give an opinion, David.

David: I think we're both too tired, that's all. In the evenings we're both too tired to talk. And Barbara . . . she never allows me to suggest anything about the house or about the kids. We always have the same arguments. She has her own opinions and that's it. Last night we had another fight. She's forbidden the kids to ride their bikes to school.

Dr. Sisters: Why?

David: She thinks they're too young to ride in the traffic. But I think they should. She always complains about picking them up at school. But they can't be tied to their mother's apron strings all their lives, can they?

Exercise 1

"Barbara's sister advised *them* to go . . ."
There are fifteen sentences like this. Underline them or write them out.

Exercise 2

They're very tired. They can't talk.
They're too tired to talk.
Continue.
1. They're very young. They shouldn't ride bikes to school.
2. He's very old. He can't go to work.
3. We were very surprised. We couldn't say anything.
4. She's very sick. She shouldn't go out.

A FUNNY THING HAPPENED TO ME...

A funny thing happened to me last Friday. I'd gone into Chicago to do some shopping. I wanted to get some Christmas presents, and I needed to find a book for my psych course (I'm a junior at Northwestern University in Evanston). I had gotten to the city early, so by early afternoon I'd bought everything that I wanted. Anyway, I'm not crazy about downtown Chicago—all the noise and traffic and strange people—and I'd made plans for that night. I just wanted to get in my car and drive home before the rush hour, but I felt really tired. I decided that I had time for a cup of coffee and a short rest. I bought a *Tribune* and went into a small cafeteria near the garage where I had parked my car. I got a cup of coffee and a package of doughnuts—glazed doughnuts. I'm crazy about glazed doughnuts. There were plenty of empty tables, and I found one near the window. I sat down and started the crossword puzzle in the paper. I always enjoy doing crossword puzzles.

A few minutes later a woman sat down across from me at my table. That surprised me because there were several empty tables. There was nothing strange about her except that she was very tall. In fact, she looked like a typical businesswoman—you know, conservative suit, briefcase—even a tie. I didn't say anything; I just kept doing the crossword. Suddenly she reached across the table, opened my package of doughnuts, took one out, dunked it in her coffee, and began to eat it. I couldn't believe my eyes! I was too shocked to say anything. Anyway, I didn't want to make a scene, so I decided to ignore it. I always avoid trouble if I can. I just took a doughnut myself and went back to my crossword.

When the woman took a second doughnut I didn't make a sound.

I pretended to be very interested in the puzzle. A few minutes later I casually put out my hand, took the last doughnut, and glanced at the woman. She was staring at me furiously. I nervously started eating the doughnut and decided to leave. I was ready to get up and go when the woman suddenly pushed back her chair, stood up, and hurried out of the cafeteria. I felt very relieved and decided to wait for two or three minutes before going myself. I finished my coffee, folded my newspaper, and stood up. And there, on the table, where my paper had been, was my package of doughnuts.

Look at this:

"I'd gone into Chicago to *do* some shopping."
"I always enjoy *doing* crossword puzzles."
"I didn't want to *make* a scene."
"I didn't *make* a sound."

Do	Make
shopping	a scene
work	plans
homework	an offer
housework	a suggestion
the cleaning	a decision
the dishes	a bed
gardening	an effort
something	an excuse
interesting	a mistake
a good job	a noise
business	a (phone) call
errands	a profit
a favor	dinner
a puzzle	trouble
	a list

Exercise

I always do my homework.
I made my bed this morning.
Write ten sentences, five with *do* and five with *make*.

Unit 10

POLITE REQUESTS

Benny Goldman used to be a popular comedian on American radio. He's nearly 70 now, but he still performs at hotels in the Catskill Mountains and other resorts in the Northeastern United States. He's on stage now at Borshsinger's Hotel in Monticello, a town in the Catskills.

Well, good evening, ladies and gentlemen—and others! It's nice to be back in Monticello at Borshsinger's again. I have to say that; I say it every night. I said it last night. The only trouble was that I was at Marco's Palace in Atlantic City. I thought the audience looked confused! Actually, I remember Monticello very well. Really! You know the first time I came here was in the 1930s. I was very young and very shy (Thank you, Mother). You can't believe that, can you? You can't imagine me either young or shy, but I was—very young and very shy. Anyway, the first Saturday night I was in Monticello I decided to go to a dance, but not at a fancy hotel like Borshsinger's. I told you I was very young and very shy. I forgot to add "very poor." Were any of you ever poor? Or young? Then maybe you remember the old Majestic Ballroom on Empire State Street. There's a parking lot there now. It

was a wonderful place, always full of beautiful girls—the ballroom, not the parking lot. Of course, most of them are grandmothers now. Oh, were you there too, dear? I was too shy to ask anyone to dance. So I sat down at a table, and I thought I'd watch for a while—you know, see how the other guys did it. At the next table there was a pretty girl in a blue dress. She'd come in with a friend, but her friend was dancing with someone. Some dude came over to her, really spiffy-looking, wearing a blue suit and a fancy silk tie. Well, he walked over to her and said, "Excuse me. May I have the pleasure of the next dance?" She looked up at him (she had beautiful big blue eyes) and said, "Hmm? What did you say?" So he said, "I wonder if you would be kind enough to dance with me—uh—if you don't mind." "Oh. No, but thank you anyway," she replied.

A few minutes later this other turkey showed up. He had on a tweed sport coat and a bow tie and a little mustache. He gave her this big smile and said, "Would you please have the next dance with me?" "Pardon?" she said. I thought to myself, "She's a little deaf—or maybe she hasn't washed her ears recently."

"Would you mind having the next dance with me?" he said, a little nervously this time. "Oh. No thanks. I'm finishing my lemonade," she replied. "Wow!" I thought, "This looks really tough."

Then another fellow came over. He was very good looking—you know, wavy blonde teeth and bright white

hair. Oops, I mean bright white teeth and wavy blonde hair. "May I ask you something?" he said very politely. "Certainly you may," she answered. "Can I—I mean, could I—uh—*may* I have the next dance with you?" "I'm sorry," she said. "My feet are killing me. I've been standing up all day at the store." By now, I was terrified. I mean she'd said no to all of them! Then this other character thought he'd give it a try.

"Would you like to dance?" he said. "What?" she replied. She was a very pretty girl, but I didn't think much of her voice! "Do you want to dance?" he said. She looked straight at him. "No," she said. That's all—"No." Well, I decided to go home. I was wearing an old jacket and an even older pair of pants, and nobody ever accused me of being good looking! Just as I was walking past her table, she smiled. "Uh—dance?" I said. "Thank you. I'd love to." she replied. And that was that! It's our forty-fifth anniversary next week.

Exercise 1
Go through and underline all the "requests." How many are there?

Exercise 2
There are six words that mean "man." What are they?

Exercise 3
Find the expressions that mean:
1. expensive and elaborate
2. a short time
3. appeared
4. unable to hear well
5. difficult, hard
6. handsome
7. make an attempt

A: Mike?
B: Yeah?
A: Close the door, will you? It's freezing in here.
B: Sure. I'm sorry.

shut the window/cold
open the door/very hot

C: Karen?
D: Hmm?
C: Lend me 50 cents. I left my purse in the office.
D: Oh, O.K. Here.
C: Thanks.

$5/wallet $1/handbag

E: Excuse me. Could you pass me the sugar?
F: Of course. There you are.
E: Thank you very much.

cream   salt   pepper

G: Do you need some help?
H: Oh, thank you. Would you mind putting my suitcase up on the rack?
G: Not at all. There you go.
H: Oh, thank you so much. You're very kind.

bag/under the seat
shopping bag/rack

I: Excuse me. It's stuffy in here. Do you mind if I open the window?
J: No, I don't mind at all. I'd like some fresh air too.

cold/close/cold too
feel hot/open/stuffy too

K: Excuse me, Lorraine. Could I ask you something?
L: Sure, Wendy. What is it?
K: Can I have the day off next Friday?
L: Well, we're very busy now. Is it important?
K: Yeah, it is, really. It's my cousin's wedding.
L: Oh, well, of course you can!

Tuesday/sister
Wednesday/nephew
Thursday/niece

M: Can I help you, ma'am?
N: I beg your pardon?
M: Can I help you, ma'am?
N: Oh. No, no thanks. I'm just looking.

Sir/Pardon?
Miss/Excuse me?

O: Good morning.
P: Good morning. I wonder if you can help me. I'm looking for a Christmas present for my father.
O: Have you thought about a nice tie?
P: Hmm . . . maybe. Could you show me some of your ties?

wedding/cousin/some towels
birthday/mother/scarf

Q: Excuse me.
R: Yes?
Q: I wonder if you'd mind handing me one of those cans of peas—on the top shelf. I can't reach it.
R: Oh, sure. There you are.
Q: Thank you very much.

box of cornflakes   package of pasta
roll of paper towels   bottle of oil

A TRIP TO LOS ANGELES

James Hall has a new job with Orange Computers · in Philadelphia. He's 23 and just out of college. As part of his training he has to spend six weeks at company headquarters near Los Angeles. It's his first business trip, and he's packing his suitcase. He lives with his parents, and his mother is helping him.

Mrs. Hall: Jimmy, haven't you finished packing yet?

James: No, Mom, but it's all right. There isn't much to do.

Mrs. Hall: Well, I'll give you a hand. Oh. There isn't much room left. Is there anywhere to put your shaving kit?

James: Yeah, sure. It'll go in here. Now, I have three more shirts to pack. They'll go on top, but there's another pair of shoes to get in. I don't know where to put them.

Mrs. Hall: Put them here, one on each side. There. O.K. I think we can close it now.

James: O. K. Where's the tag?

Mrs. Hall: What tag, dear?

James: The name tag that the airline gave me to put on the suitcase. Oh, here it is.

Mrs. Hall: Now, do you have the key?

James: What key?

Mrs. Hall: The key to lock the suitcase, of course.

James: It's in the lock, Mom. Don't make such a production. There's nothing to worry about. There's plenty of time.

Mrs. Hall: Have you forgotten anything?

James: I hope not.

Mrs. Hall: And you have a safe pocket for your traveler's checks?

James: Yes, they're in my inside coat pocket.

Mrs. Hall: Do you have a book to read on the plane?

James: Yes, it's in my briefcase.

Mrs. Hall: What about small change to make phone calls?

James: Check. I have a pocketful of coins.

Mrs. Hall: And is everything all arranged?

James: What do you mean?

Mrs. Hall: Well, is there someone to meet you in Los Angeles?

James: No, Mom. I'll rent a car and go to a motel near the Orange office. They suggested the Newport Beach Holiday Inn.

Mrs. Hall: Do you have a reservation?

James: I hope so. I asked them to make it—the motel reservation, I mean. (I reserved the car myself.)

Mrs. Hall: Well, you've taken care of everything. I don't know why I'm worrying. Take care of yourself and be good. Call us tonight.

James: Thanks, Mom. I will.

Mrs. Hall: Oh, I nearly forgot! Here's some gum to chew on the plane— you know, when it's coming down. It's sugarless.

James: Oh, Mom. Don't worry. I'll be all right. I'll see you next month.

Exercise 1
James lives in Teaneck, New Jersey, across the Hudson River from New York City. His mother drove him to a bus stop in Teaneck. He took a bus to New York, then a subway train to Kennedy Airport, and finally a plane to Los Angeles. How can you get to your nearest airport? What is the best way for you to get there?

Exercise 2
James made a list. Look at it.
He remembered to pack his shirts.
He forgot to pack his raincoat.

Exercise 3
Think about the clothes you would pack for a two-week trip to New York or Boston in the spring. Imagine that you have just been on a plane and the airline has lost your suitcase. Make a list of the clothes you had in your suitcase.
one dark blue wool sweater
one brown leather belt

FLYING TO L.A.

At the airport

James is at the Pan American Terminal at Kennedy Airport. He's already checked in. He's been through the security check, and he's gone to the gate to wait for his flight. Listen to the announcements. Look at the screen, look at the example, and complete the chart in the same way.

PAN AM			
FLIGHT	DESTINATION	GATE	DEPARTS
932	Syracuse	14	3:25
217			
558			
563			
67			
811			

In flight

James is now on the plane. Listen to the announcements, and answer these questions.
1. What's the pilot's name?
   What are they waiting for?
   How long will the delay be?
   When will they arrive in Los Angeles?
2. What kind of plane is it?
   How fast is it going?
   Where is the plane?
   How hot is it in Los Angeles?
   What's the weather like?
   Why should the passengers keep their seat belts fastened?
3. What's the plane beginning to do?
   What should the passengers do?
   When can they start smoking again?
4. What should the passengers do?
   When can they stand up?
   Who should they see if they have questions?

Dinner on the plane

Flight Attendant: Are you having dinner, sir?
James: Yeah—uh—yes, thanks.
Flight Attendant: We have a choice today of chicken or steak.
James: I'll take the steak. Could I get some red wine with that?
Flight Attendant: The beverage cart will come down this aisle in a few minutes. You can order your wine then.
James: Thank you. Is there a charge for the wine?
Flight Attendant: Yes. The soft drinks are free.

In flight questionnaire

Flight Attendant: Excuse me, sir. Would you mind filling out this questionnaire?
James: What's it about?
Flight Attendant: We want to learn more about our passengers so we can provide the best service.
James: Sure, I'll fill it out.

PAN AM PASSENGER QUESTIONNAIRE

Please take a few minutes to fill out this questionnaire and return it to your flight attendant. Thank you.
Date ___/___/___   Flight No. _____
From _____   To _____
How many trips do you make in the U.S. in a year?
1 - 2 ☐   3 - 5 ☐   6 - 9 ☐   More ☐
Business ☐   Leisure ☐   Other _____
What cities do you travel to most frequently?
Chicago ☐   New York ☐   Los Angeles ☐
Houston ☐   Other _____
Why are you flying Pan Am today?
Best schedule ☐   Past experience ☐
Travel agent's recommendations ☐
Advertising ☐   Other _____

Auto rental

James: You have no record of my reservation? What do I do now?
Attendant: We have several cars, sir. Let's fill out this form. O.K. Hall, James. Address?
James: 427 Battle Terrace, Teaneck, New Jersey 07666
Attendant: Are you here on business or pleasure?
James: Business.
Attendant: How long will you need the car?
James: I don't know for sure. Put down two days. The company might pay for more.
Attendant: All right. Let me see your driver's license and a major credit card.

MONEY

Money is used for buying or selling goods, for measuring value and for storing wealth. Almost every society now has a money economy based on coins and paper bills of one kind or another. However, this has not always been true. In primitive societies a system of barter was used. Barter was a system of direct exchange of goods. Somebody could exchange a sheep, for example, for anything in the market-place that they considered to be of equal value. Barter, however, was a very unsatisfactory system because people's precise needs seldom coincided. People needed a more practical system of exchange, and various money systems developed based on goods which the members of a society recognized as having value. Cattle, grain, teeth, shells, feathers, skulls, salt, elephant tusks, and tobacco have all been used. Precious metals gradually took over because, when made into coins, they were portable, durable, recognizable, and divisible into larger and smaller units of value.

A coin is a piece of metal, usually disc-shaped, which bears lettering, designs or numbers showing its value. Until the eighteenth and nineteenth centuries, coins were given monetary worth based on the exact amount of metal contained in them, but most modern coins are based on face value—the value that governments choose to give them, irrespective of the actual metal content. Coins have been made of gold (Au), silver (Ag), copper (Cu), aluminum (Al), nickel (Ni), lead (Pb), zinc (Zn), plastic and in China even from pressed tea leaves. Most governments now issue paper money in the form of bills, which are really "promises to pay." Paper money is obviously easier to handle and much more convenient in the modern world. Checks and credit cards are being used increasingly, and it is possible to imagine a world where "money" in the form of coins and paper currency will no longer be used. Even today, in the United States, many places, especially filling stations will not accept cash at night for security reasons.

Exercise 1
Find expressions which mean:
1. A place to buy gas
2. A place where goods are bought and sold
3. The period between 1801 and 1900
4. The bony structure of the head
5. Round and flat in shape
6. An exchange of goods for other goods

Exercise 2
Find words which mean:
1. Can be divided
2. Lasts a long time
3. Can be carried
4. Can be recognized

Exercise 3
Put these words in the correct places in the sentences below:
coins/cash/currency/money
1. The ... of Japan is the yen.
2. She has a lot of ... in her bank account.
3. It costs $20 if you're paying in ... It'll be more if you pay by check.
4. Can you change this dollar bill into ... for the coffee machine?

Exercise 4
Money is used for buying goods.
This sentence means: *You can buy goods with it.*
Write similar sentences which mean:
1. You can measure value with it.
2. You can store wealth with it.
3. You can sell things for it.

Exercise 5
Money is used for buying and selling goods.
People use money for buying and selling goods.
Change these sentences in the same way:
1. A system of barter was used.
2. Cattle, grain, and tobacco have all been used.
3. Paper currency will no longer be used.
4. Checks and credit cards are being used.

Exercise 6
Somebody could exchange a sheep.
A sheep could be exchanged.
Change these sentences in the same way:
1. People needed a more practical system.
2. Most governments now issue paper money in the form of bills.
3. Filling stations will not accept cash at night.

Exercise 7
Money *is used for buying things.*
Shampoo *is used for washing your hair.*
Make sentences with: knife/pen/key/camera/suitcase/toothpaste/detergent/wallet/hair dryer.

Exercise 8
A place where you can fill your gas tank is a *filling station.*
Complete these sentences:
1. A special room where you can wait is a ...
2. A pill which helps you to sleep is a ...
3. An account on which you can write checks is a ...
4. A glove which boxers wear is a ...
5. Oil you can cook with is ...
6. A pool where you can swim is a ...
7. Special liquid you can wash dishes with is ...

Unit 14

MONEY, MONEY, MONEY

Bargaining

Sally Grooms is at a flea market in a small Pennsylvania town. She's just seen a glass bowl at one of the stands. She collects American glass objects made during the Depression of the 1930s. She's interested in buying the bowl. Listen to her conversation with the owner of the stand, and answer these questions.

1. How much does he say it's worth?
2. How much is he asking for it?
3. What does "buck" mean?
4. He suggests four different prices. Write them down.
5. She makes four offers. Write them down.

Some sayings in English about money:

" Neither a borrower nor a lender be. "

From Hamlet *by William Shakespeare.*

Have you ever borrowed money from anyone? Who from? How much?

Have you ever lent money to anyone? Who to? How much?

Are you in debt at the moment? (i.e., do you owe anyone any money?)

Does anyone owe you any money? Who? How much?

" A penny saved is a penny earned. "

Benjamin Franklin

Do you save money? Are you saving for anything at the moment? What?

Do you keep your money (a) in the bank? (b) in a safe? (c) in a book? (d) under the bed? (e) in the refrigerator?

Do you have a bank account? Do you have a checking account or a savings account? What's the interest rate? If your account was overdrawn, how much would the bank charge you?

" Buy now; pay later. "

Have you bought anything on credit? What? Did you pay a deposit? Do you think it's a good idea?

Do you have a credit card? Which one? (Visa? American Express? Diner's Club? Mastercard?)

When you pay cash, do you ask for a discount? Do you usually get it?

" All progress is based upon a universal innate desire on the part of every organism to live beyond its income. "

Samuel Butler

Do you spend more than you earn or less than you earn?

Do you have a budget for your money?

Do you keep a record of your expenses? Why?

" A fool and his money are soon parted. "

Where do you carry your spending money?
(a) in a purse (b) in a wallet (c) in a pocket

If you keep it in a pocket, which pocket do you keep it in?
(a) inside pocket of coat/jacket
(b) breast pocket of coat/jacket
(c) side pocket of coat/jacket
(d) back pocket of pants
(e) front pocket of pants

Have you ever had your pocket picked?

When you stay in a hotel, do you hide your money? Where?
(a) in your suitcase (b) under the mattress (c) in the pillow (d) in a book (e) somewhere else

Is gambling legal or illegal in your city/state/country? Do people bet? What do they bet on?
(a) cards (b) horse racing (c) dog racing (d) football/soccer/other sport (e) boxing (f) national lottery (g) something else

" The customer is always right. "

Have you bought anything this week? What?

What did it cost? Was it worth it?

Was it new or used?

Was it a bargain? Did you get a receipt?

Have you ever returned anything you had bought? What? Where?

Did you get your money back, a new article, a different article, or credit for a future purchase?

INSIDE STORY

"ECHO" REPORTER MISSING IN MANDANGAN WAR

PETTYVILLE, MANDANGA, May 12. Julie Mendoza, the veteran "Daily Echo" war correspondent, who is covering the civil war in Mandanga, has been reported missing.

Mendoza was last seen yesterday morning driving her jeep near the front line. The vehicle was found last night, but there was no sign of Mendoza. It is possible that she was ambushed and captured by rebel forces. Mendoza has been a war correspondent for many years and has covered a number of conflicts in different parts of the world. She has won two Pulitzer prizes for her

MENDOZA FREE

PETTYVILLE, MANDANGA, May 22. "Echo" war correspondent Julie Mendoza walked into a government forces camp this morning after spending ten days with Free Mandanga rebels. She appeared well and unharmed. She spoke to her brother and this paper by telephone before she was taken to her

IBC Evening News

The fighting between government and rebel forces in Mandanga continues tonight, with no end in sight. The only good news from that war-torn country was that war correspondent Julie Mendoza is alive and well. She was missing for ten days, but this morning she appeared at a government forces camp. We go to Pettyville for a report from Hank McLaughlin.

McLaughlin: Julie Mendoza is with me here at the Interhemisphere Hotel. After ten days with Mandangan rebels, she returned to Pettyville today. Julie, can you tell us how you were captured?

Mendoza: I was on my way to a vil-

lage near the front line. I came around a bend in the road, and there was a tree lying across the road. I managed to stop in time. Suddenly, armed men appeared on all sides!

McLaughlin: What did you do?

Mendoza: What would anybody do? I put my hands up! Anyway, they made me get out of my jeep; then they made me lie down on the ground. I thought, "This is it. They're going to shoot me!"

McLaughlin: What happened next?

Mendoza: Well, they searched me and the jeep. I didn't have any weapons, just a camera and a tape recorder. It's funny—they let me keep them. They tied my hands together and blindfolded me. Then they made me get in the back of a truck and lie under some sacks. I have no idea where they took me, except that it was a pretty big training camp. I was there for ten days.

McLaughlin: Were you treated well?

Mendoza: More or less. They let me walk around, and let me take pictures, but not of any of their faces. I was able to interview some of the leaders.

McLaughlin: How did you escape?

Mendoza: I didn't. They put me back

in the truck, blindfolded me again, drove for a few hours, then made me get out, and let me go.

McLaughlin: What exactly did the rebel leaders say?

Mendoza: I'll be writing about that for my readers first, Hank.

McLaughlin: Huh? Oh. Yes. This has been Hank McLaughlin reporting for IBC News in Mandanga.

MANDANGAN REBEL LEADERS PROMISE FIGHT TO DEATH

by JULIE MENDOZA

(This is the first of a three-part report written by Julie Mendoza, who spent 10 days with Mandangan rebels after her capture on May 11. The rebels forced her to go with them to their camp. However, they allowed her to keep her camera and tape recorder and to interview rebel leaders. Exclusive pictures on page 2.)

PETTYVILLE, MANDANGA, May 25. "We will fight till we win or die," declared

Exercise

When I was younger, my parents made me go to bed early.

When I was younger, my parents didn't let me go out at night.

Write true sentences about when you were younger.

PREFERENCES

A: What are you doing tomorrow night?
B: Nothing. Why?
A: Well, do you like country music?
B: Yes, I do—very much.
A: What do you like best—country western or bluegrass?
B: I like both, as a matter of fact.
A: Joe Ed Davis is playing at the Ale House. Would you like to go?
B: Yes, great! He's one of my favorites!

C: Hey, Charlene, look over here. They have a fabulous selection of designer jeans!
D: Oh, yeah! And they have my size!
C: But only Calvin Pines and Gloria Randibilts.
D: Yeah. Hmm. I don't like either one of them very much. I really wanted some Sergio Potentes.
C: But they don't have them in your size. Go ahead and try on a pair of Calvin Pines.
D: Nah. I'll wait and see if I find some Sergio Potentes somewhere else.

E: Well, have you decided yet? What do you want to see?
F: *A Moment of Peace* is on at the Arapahoe Two. I'd like to see that.
E: You would? I'd rather see *War in Space*.
F: Oh, no! The reviews were terrible.
E: I know, but it sounds like fun. *A Moment of Peace* is in French and I'd really rather not have to read subtitles.
F: Then how about *California Sunset*?
E: I'd rather not. I can't stand Steve Newman.
F: Well, you choose then.
E: Actually, I don't want to see any of them. I'd much rather stay home and watch TV.

G: What are you up for?
H: I don't know. There isn't much choice, is there?
G: No, not really. What would you rather have? Chicken a la King or spaghetti and meatballs?
H: I can't make up my mind. Uh—I'd just like a tuna fish sandwich.
G: We can look at the regular menu, if you'd like.
H: Nah, it's not worth it. I'll have the spaghetti.

This week in Denver

Jazz, Rock, Pop

★ **Blaze Foley** and the **Ramblers** (country and western) Billy's (861- 9540), Wed. & Thurs.

★ **Joe Ed Davis** and the **Harris County Line Band**, (bluegrass) Ale House (499-3773), Tues. — Thurs.

★ **Huey Lewis and the News** (Rock) Sharon Hall (861-4500), Fri. midnight

★ **Pat Benatar** in concert. Memorial Coliseum (499-5000), Sat. 8 p.m.

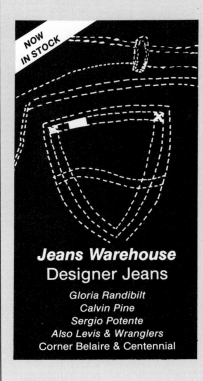

NOW IN STOCK

Jeans Warehouse
Designer Jeans

Gloria Randibilt
Calvin Pine
Sergio Potente
Also Levis & Wranglers
Corner Belaire & Centennial

Movies

Arapahoe 1 & 2
Halloween XII (PG)
A Moment of Peace (R) (Fr., Eng. subtitles)

Baronet
California Sunset (PG)
Steve Newman,
Gloria Gusto

Classic Cinema
Casablanca (no rating) Ingrid Bergman, Humphrey Bogart; and
Play It Again, Sam (G) Woody Allen

Paramount
War in Space (G) Raquel Evans, Chase Carson, Milly Thompson

Ritz
The Day We Had (R) Muriel Street, Jeremy Steel

TONIGHT'S TOPIC: 42ND STREET

"Good evening. I'm Harry Barber and this is Radio Station WLFM. Our topic tonight on 'Call In' is New York's 42nd Street, particularly the Times Square area. It's the most crime-filled area in the city. It's a place for drug dealers and alcoholics, action movies and pornography. It's inhabited by all kinds of street people from bag ladies and homeless kids to street corner orators and junkies. And it's becoming more and more dangerous. What should the city do? What do you listeners think? Call in. Maybe you can suggest some solutions."

"Hi, Harry. My name's Stuart Amos. I think the city should spend time doing something about it. They ought to redevelop the whole area. They ought to get rid of the pornography. I stopped going to that area a long time ago because I was really afraid that I'd get mugged or something. I mean, you never see a cop down there. And the Times Square subway station is full of strange characters. Somebody ought to do something. It's disgraceful."

"Thanks, Stuart, for your opinion. Now would someone call in and tell us what the city should do?"

"Hello, Harry. I'm Hilda Diaz. I agree with Mr. Amos. When I was young, I used to go to Times Square with my parents. But I wouldn't take my kids there now. There are too many bad influences like stores that specialize in pornography or weapons. And you always hear foul language in the street. Also it's the theater district. I love the theater even though it's so expensive. But I have to take public transportation to get there, and I won't risk my life taking the subway when I leave the theater at night. So I never go. Anyway, people have been talking about these problems for ten years and nothing has been done. We'd better not spend another minute talking about it. We'd better do something about it soon!"

"Right, Hilda. I'm sure we all sympathize with you. But lots of people think the city had better do something. Isn't there anyone who can offer a concrete solution? Call in, please."

"Harry, I'm Andrea Martin. I'd like to mention the positive side. 42nd Street from Eighth Avenue to Eleventh Avenue used to be just as bad—full of crumbling buildings and dirty, rundown fast food restaurants. In the past few years the city has redeveloped the area. It's become a new theater district. And it's not so expensive, so everyone can go to the theater there. There are also lovely restaurants and nice stores. We ought to give credit to the city for doing this."

"Thanks, Andrea. But don't you think the city ought to do more? O.K. Who's our next caller?"

"Harry, my name's Milton Kramer. I'm the chairman of the Committee to Redevelop 42nd Street. Obviously you haven't heard of this project, so I'll tell you and your listeners about it. In the next six years we plan to renovate the street's historic theaters, redesign the Times Square subway station, and build a 560-room hotel and four new office buildings. This will eliminate the lawless elements in the area and bring in theater-goers, office workers, and tourists. So you see, a solution already exists. And Harry, I think you'd better do your homework before you ask questions that already have answers."

Exercise
Find words which mean:
1. people who drink too much
2. public speakers
3. clearly
4. share the same feelings
5. falling apart
6. make over
7. take a chance
8. homeless woman who carries belongings in shopping bags
9. shameful
10. without a place to live

NIGHT FLIGHT

"This is your captain, John Cook speaking. Our estimated time of arrival in Anchorage is one a.m., so we've got a long flight ahead of us. I hope you enjoy it. Our flight attendants will be serving dinner shortly. Thank you."

It was Christmas Eve 1959, and the beginning of another routine flight. The flight attendants started preparing the food trays. A few of the passengers were trying to get some sleep, but most of them were reading. There was nothing to see from the windows except the vast blackness of the winter night. The plane was nearly full. A lot of the passengers were traveling home to spend Christmas with their families. The flight attendants started serving dinner.

It was a smooth and quiet flight. The flight attendants had finished picking up the trays, and they were in the galley putting things away when the first buzzers sounded. One of the flight attendants went along the aisle to check. When he came back he looked surprised. "It's amazing," he said. "Even on a smooth flight like this two people have been sick."

Twenty minutes later nearly half the passengers were ill—dramatically ill. Several were moaning and groaning, some were doubled up in pain, and two were unconscious. Fortunately there was a doctor on board, and he was helping the flight attendants. He came to the galley and said, "I'd better speak to the pilot. This is a severe case of food poisoning. I think we'd better land as soon as possible." "What caused it?" asked one of the flight attendants. "Well," replied the doctor, "I had the beef for dinner, and I'm fine. The passengers who chose the fish are sick." The flight attendant led him to the cockpit. She tried to open the door. "I think it's jammed," she said. The doctor helped her to push it open. The captain was lying behind

the door. He was unconscious. The copilot was slumped across the controls, and the engineer was trying to revive him.

The doctor quickly examined the two men. "They just collapsed," said the engineer. "I don't feel too good myself." "Can you land the plane?" said the doctor. "Me? No, I'm not a pilot. We've got to revive them!" he replied. "The plane's on automatic pilot. We're O.K. for a couple of hours." "I don't know," said the doctor. "They could be out for a long time." "I'd better contact ground control," said the engineer. The doctor turned to the flight attendant. "Maybe you should make an announcement and try to find out if there's a pilot on board." "We can't do that!" she said. "It'll cause a general panic." "Then how are we going to get this thing down?" said the doctor.

Suddenly the flight attendant remembered something. "One of the passengers ... I overheard him saying that he'd been a pilot in the war. I'll get him." She found the man and asked him to come to the galley. "Didn't you say you used to be a pilot?" she asked. "Yes ... why? The pilot's all right, isn't he?" She led him to the cockpit. They explained the situation to him. "You mean, you want me to fly the plane?" he said. "You must be joking. I was a pilot, but I flew single-engined fighter planes, and that was fifteen years ago. This thing's got four engines!"

"Isn't there anybody else?" he asked. "I'm afraid not," said the flight attendant. The man sat down at the controls. His hands were shaking slightly. The engineer connected him to Air Traffic Control. They told him to keep flying on automatic pilot toward Anchorage and to wait for further instructions from an experienced pilot. An hour later the lights of Anchorage appeared on the horizon. He could see the lights of the runway shining brightly by a lake. Air Traffic Control told him to keep circling until the fuel gauge registered almost empty. This gave him a chance to get used to handling the controls. In the cabin the flight attendants and the doctor were busy attending to the sick. Several people were unconscious. The plane circled for over half an hour. The passengers had begun to realize that something was wrong. "What's going on? Why don't we land?" shouted a

middle aged man. "My wife's sick. We've got to get her to the hospital!" A woman began sobbing quietly. At last the plane started its descent. Suddenly there was a bump which shook the plane. "We're all going to die!" screamed a man. Even the flight attendants looked worried as panic began to spread through the plane. "It's all right!" someone said. "The pilot just lowered the landing gear, that's all." As the plane approached the runway they could see fire trucks and ambulances speeding alongside the runway with their lights flashing. There was a tremendous thump as the wheels hit the tarmac, bounced twice, raced along the runway, and screeched to a halt. The first airport truck was there in seconds. "That was nearly a perfect landing. Well done!" shouted the control tower. "Thanks," said the man. "Any chance of a job?"

THE CURIO SHOP

Anita Alvarado and Steve Weaver are antique dealers. They have a very successful business. They travel around the country buying antique furniture and paintings from flea markets, junk stores, and elderly people. Then they sell them at their store in Greenwich Village, a fashionable part of New York City. Today they're in a small town in South Carolina. Steve has just come out of a little curio shop, and he seems very excited.

Steve: Anita, we're in luck! There's a painting in there, a landscape. It's a good one. I thought it might be valuable, so I took a good look at the signature. It isn't very clear. I think it may be a Winslow Homer.

Anita: A Winslow Homer?! It can't be! They're all in museums. They're worth a fortune!

Steve: Well, someone found one a couple of years ago. This might be another one. It's dirty, and it isn't in very good condition.

Anita: How much do you think it's worth?

Steve: I don't know. It may be worth a million; it might even be worth more!

Anita: Be careful, Steve. We'd better use the old trick.

Steve: Yeah, right. There's a chair in the window. It must be worth about twenty dollars. I'll offer the old lady a hundred bucks for it. She'll be so happy that she won't think about the painting.

Anita: Don't say you want the painting; say you want the frame. O.K.?

Steve: Fine, you'd better wait in the van. I'd rather do this on my own.

Anita: Uh . . . Steve, check the signature before you give her a hundred bucks for the chair.

Steve: Don't worry, Anita. I know what I'm doing.

Mrs. Venable: I'll be with you in a minute.

Steve: I'm interested in that chair in the window.

Mrs. Venable: What? That old thing? It's been there for years!

Steve: It has? Uh . . . it's very nice. I think it could be Victorian.

Mrs. Venable: Really?

Steve: Yes, I think I'm right. I've seen one or two other chairs like it. I think I could get a good price for that in New York. I'll offer you a hundred dollars.

Mrs. Venable: A hundred dollars! You must be out of your mind!

Steve: No, no. It's a fair price.

Mrs. Venable: Well, then, it's yours.

Steve: There you are then, a hundred dollars. Good-bye. Oh, by the way, that painting's in a nice frame.

Mrs. Venable: It's a nice picture, honey. Late nineteenth century, I've heard.

Steve: Oh, no . . . no, it can't be. I've seen lots like it. It must be twentieth century. There's no market for them. Still, I could use the frame.

Mrs. Venable: All right. How much will you give me for it?

Steve: Uh . . . how about forty dollars?

Mrs. Venable: Oh, no, honey. It must be worth more than that. It came from the big house on the hill.

Steve: It did? Let me have another look at it. Yes, the frame really is nice. I'll give you two hundred.

Mrs. Venable: Oh my, I don't know what to do. You see, I like that painting myself.

Steve: All right, two hundred and fifty. That's my final offer.

Mrs. Venable: Let's say . . . two seventy-five?

Steve: O.K. It's a deal.

Mrs. Venable: Shall I wrap it up for you?

Steve: No, no. I have the van outside. It was nice doing business with you. Good-bye!

Mrs. Venable: Bye-bye, honey. Thank you. You come back to see us, you hear?

Mrs. Venable: Beauregard?
Mr. Venable: Yes, darling?
Mrs. Venable: I've sold another one of your imitation Winslow Homers. You'd better bring another one downstairs, if the paint's dry. The young gentleman who bought it seemed very happy with it.

Look at this:

I'm certain . . . I'm almost certain . . .	It must be . . .
I think it's possible . . .	It could be . . . It may be . . .
I think it's possible . . . (but a little less possible than "may")	It might be . . .
I think it's almost impossible . . .	It can't be . . .
I think it's impossible . . .	It couldn't be . . .

NOISY NEIGHBORS

Harriet: Pssst! Ozzie! Ozzie! Wake up!

Ozzie: Huh? What? What's the matter? It can't be seven o'clock already!

Harriet: No. It's half past one. It's those people next door again. Listen!

Ozzie: Oh, yeah. They must be having another party.

Harriet: Listen to that! They must be waking up the whole block. And they have three young children. They couldn't be sleeping through that racket. It's disgusting! Somebody should call the police! Ozzie, wake up!

Ozzie: Huh? I wasn't asleep, dear. They're all laughing. They must be having a good time. They never invite us, do they?

Harriet: Ozzie!

Ozzie: Yes, dear. What is it now?

Harriet: Listen! They must be leaving.

Ozzie: Thank goodness for that! Maybe we'll get some sleep.

Harriet: I hope so. It's nearly three o'clock. Goodnight, dear. Oh, no! Now they're having a fight.

Ozzie: I'm not surprised. They always have fights after parties.

Harriet: Uh, oh! They must be throwing the dishes again.

Ozzie: No, I think that was a vase dear, or maybe the TV set—or both! They'll be sorry in the morning.

Harriet: Ozzie! Wake up!

Ozzie: Huh? Oh, what's that banging?

Harriet: He couldn't be hammering at this time of night.

Ozzie: What time is it?

Harriet: Four o'clock. What could they be doing at four o'clock in the morning?

Ozzie: I don't hear any voices. Go back to sleep, Harriet dear.

Harriet: Ozzie! Listen. There's someone in the backyard next door.

Ozzie: Huh? It must be the garbage man.

Harriet: No, it can't be. It's too early. It's only a quarter to five. Who could it be? I'd better take a look. Ooh! It's Howard Kennedy, and he's carrying a shovel.

Ozzie: Really? You don't think he's killed her, do you?

Harriet: Well, we haven't heard her voice for a while. No, she's probably sleeping.

Ozzie: But what could he be doing at this time of night?

Harriet: If he has killed her, he might be burying the body!

Ozzie: What?! You don't think so, do you?

Harriet: Well, he couldn't be planting tomatoes, could he? Do you think I should call the police?

Ozzie: No. Why don't you ask him what he's doing first!

Harriet: Hello there, Howard. You're up bright and early this morning.

Howard: I haven't been to bed yet. We had a party last night. I hope we didn't keep you awake.

Harriet: Oh, no, no. We didn't hear a thing, nothing at all. I slept like a log.

Howard: Well, it was a pretty noisy party. My wife knocked over the kids' tropical fish tank while we were cleaning up. The poor fish died. I'm just burying them before the kids wake up.

Exercise

What do you think your parents/ brothers/sisters/friends are doing right now.

If you think you know what they are doing, answer with:
They must be doing this.
They couldn't be doing that.
They're probably doing this.

If you don't know, use:
They could/may/might be doing this.
or:
They're possibly doing this.

What about the President of the U.S./ the Queen of England/the students in the class next door/the principal of the school/a famous movie or TV star/a famous sports celebrity.

A SPARKLING CAMP

It's a Friday afternoon in June at the Tukabatchee Summer Camp. The camp counselors are supposed to be working, but they aren't. The camp has to be ready for the first summer campers. They'll arrive tomorrow. The counselors have had lunch, and they're taking it easy in the counselors' lounge. The camp director has just opened the door. He's brought the duty roster with him, so he knows exactly what each of them should be doing.

Director: Hey, what's going on here?

Exercise 1
Look at Terri in the picture. Ask and answer about the other counselors.

1. *What's she doing?*
   She's lying on the sofa.
   She's smoking.
   She's watching TV.
2. *Should she be smoking?*
   No, she shouldn't.
   Should she be cutting the grass?
   Yes, she should.
3. *What should she be doing?*
   She should be cutting the grass.
   What shouldn't she be doing?

TUKABATCHEE SUMMER CAMP
"A Sparkling Camp by the Sparkling Water"
Counselors' Duties

Date: June 24

Counselor	Duty
Terri B.	cut grass
Kevin G.	paint canoes
Linda H.	clean swimming pool
Shawn M.	mark volleyball courts
Michelle S.	straighten up crafts room

She shouldn't be lying on the sofa.
She shouldn't be smoking.
She shouldn't be watching TV.

Exercise 2
Terri ought to be cutting the grass.
She ought not to be smoking.
Write similar sentences about the other counselors.

Director: Terri! What are you doing?
Terri: I'm watching TV.
Director: And what are you supposed to be doing, Terri?
Terri: I'm not sure.
Director: Well, let me tell you, Terri. You're supposed to be cutting the grass.
Terri: Oh, right! I'm sorry. I forgot.
Director: When I come back, you'd better be cutting the grass. Do you hear me?
Terri: Yeah, yeah. I'm going.
Director: Get a move on, Terri. Remember the Tukabatchee motto: "A sparkling camp by the sparkling water."

Exercise 3
Make similar conversations between the director and the other counselors.

Look at this:

Exercise 4
Terri's cutting the grass.
She'd rather not be cutting the grass.
She'd rather be lying on the beach.
Make sentences about the other counselors.

Exercise 5
What are you doing?
What would you rather be doing?
Make five sentences.

Unit 22

MIGRATION

One of the greatest mysteries of nature is the instinct to migrate. Every year millions of creatures feel the need to move for one reason or another. Most of us have seen the arrival or departure of migrating flocks of birds. Migration, however, is not confined to birds, but can be seen in reptiles (for example, turtles, frogs), insects (butterflies, locusts), fish (eels, salmon, tuna) and mammals (reindeer, seals, lemmings, whales, bats). Many of these creatures succeed in navigating over long distances. Just how they manage to do this still remains a mystery. There are several possibilities. They may navigate by using one or more of the following:

1. The sun.
2. The stars.
3. The earth's magnetic field. (When a small bar magnet is attached to a pigeon, it is unable to navigate.)
4. A sense of smell.
5. Geographical features. (Birds flying from South America to Canada seem to follow coastlines and valleys.)
6. Changes in temperature. (Salmon can detect a change in water temperature as small as .05 of a degree F.)
7. Sound. (Whales and bats seem to use sonar.)

Experiments suggest that these navigational abilities are partly instinctive. In one famous experiment a young seabird from the British Isles was taken across the Atlantic by plane to Boston, 3,200 miles away. It was released and was back in its nest twelve and a half days later.

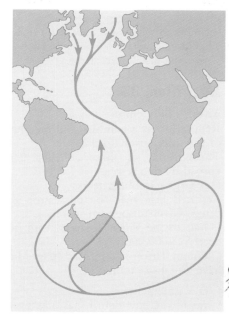

The Arctic Tern

This seabird holds the record for long-distance migration. Arctic Tern breed in northern Canada, Greenland, northern Europe, Siberia, and Alaska. In late August they set off on an 11,000-mile journey which takes them south past the western coasts of Europe and Africa to the southern tip of Africa (9,000 miles in 90 days). They then fly around to the Indian Ocean and down to Antarctica, where they spend the Antarctic summer. On the way back they sometimes make a complete circle of Antarctica before returning to their breeding grounds. The round trip is about 22,000 miles in eight months (150 miles a day when they are flying.) The Arctic Tern sees more hours of daylight than any other creature because it experiences two summers a year—one in the Arctic region and one in the Antarctic. These regions have almost constant daylight in summer. One tern, which was tagged with a ring in Norway as a chick, died in exactly the same place, twenty-seven years later. Presumably, it had made the journey twenty-seven times.

The European Freshwater Eel

European Freshwater Eels, which look like snakes but are really fish, begin and end their lives in the Sargasso Sea, southeast of Bermuda. As eggs and larvae they drift for three years towards Europe, changing both shape and color as they reach the freshwater estuaries of European rivers. They spend the next nine to nineteen years in rivers, streams, lakes, and ponds. As they approach old age they seem to return to the Sargasso Sea to spawn. Many eels which have found their way into ponds and lakes come out of the water and travel over land, slithering through damp grass. When they reach the ocean, they make their way to the Sargasso, where they spawn and die. No eels make the journey twice. The eel has an acute sense of smell, which is used for navigation in local waters, but inherited memory seems the only explanation for their migration to the Sargasso.

The Lemming

The Brown Lemming is a small mammal (4–7 inches long) found all over the northern parts of North America and Europe. Lemmings usually make short, annual migrations in the spring, traveling by night and feeding and sleeping by day. Every three or four years, however, they make much longer migrations in large numbers. The lemming population seems to change over a three or four year cycle, from one lemming per acre to between 400 and 700 lemmings per acre. Migration seems to be a method of population control and is most spectacular in the well-known "mass suicides," where thousands of lemmings plunge over cliff tops into the sea and swim until they die of exhaustion. These "mass suicides" only occur infrequently and then only in Norway where mountains touch the sea. Nobody knows what makes them do it, but there are two theories. One is that migrating lemmings cross rivers and lakes and can't tell the difference between a river and the sea. The other more interesting theory is that they are migrating towards ancient breeding grounds which existed beneath the North Sea millions of years ago, when the sea level was lower.

MURDER IN NEW ORLEANS

Part 1

John Beresford Tifton was found dead on the floor of his study in the Tifton family mansion in New Orleans. He had been shot five times. The police have been called. There are six people in the house, and they all heard the shots at about four o'clock this afternoon. The police have taken statements and made the following notes about each of the six people.

Lydia Dubois Tifton, 62

Married to John Tifton for thirty-five years.
Handicapped—has been in a wheelchair since a riding accident twelve years ago.
Had a loud argument with Ruth Ellen Potts this morning.
Told Tifton to fire Ruth Ellen.
After long argument, Tifton refused to fire her.

Lydia Tifton's statement

I was in my room. I had the old den on the first floor turned into a bedroom for me because I can't walk. I was reading. I heard the shots; there were four or five. I wheeled myself into the hall. The study door was open. Ruth Ellen was standing in the doorway screaming. Benson was standing at the French windows. The gun was on the floor by Big Daddy.

Ruth Ellen Potts, 24

Tifton's private secretary.
Young, beautiful, intelligent—works to support her sick mother.
Has worked for Tifton for a year.
Report in a gossip column in today's *Picayune Times* says she had been seen with J. D. Tifton at a new disco, The Red Parrot, near the French Quarter.
Old Tifton was very upset about it.
Threatened to fire her but didn't.

Ruth Ellen Potts's statement

I was in the living room writing some letters—actually job applications. I heard the shots and ran across the hall. The door to the study was open. There was poor, dear John—Mr. Tifton—lying in a pool of blood. I started screaming. Benson came in through the French windows; they were open. Then Lydia arrived. She didn't say a word. She just stared at me.

J.D. Tifton, 33

Tifton's only child.
Reputation as a gambler and member of the international jet set.
Thrown out of three colleges. Divorced by two wives.
Has large gambling debts.
Arrested last year for possession of drugs. Given suspended sentence.
Is heir to the Tifton fortune. Will inherit $25,000,000.
Old man Tifton had refused to let him have any more money.

J. D.'s statement

I was in the new den. I was playing a video game. Suddenly there were five shots. I thought it was Uncle Ike at target practice. Then I heard a scream. It sounded like Ruth Ellen; so I opened the connecting door to the study and saw Big Daddy lying there, Benson at the French windows, and Big Mama and Ruth Ellen together in the doorway to the hall. I couldn't believe my eyes.

Charles ("Cajun") Long, 29

Chauffer. Son of old man Tifton's ex-secretary. Often goes fishing with Dubois.
Wanted to marry Ruth Ellen Potts. Proposed to her, but she turned him down.
Has been in trouble with the police several times for fighting in bars.
Has violent temper.
Had argument with Tifton about a raise in pay earlier in the day.

Cajun Long's statement

I was working on the car. I heard shots, but old man Tifton and Ike—Mr. Dubois—have a little target practice sometimes. The police never bother them. Then I heard lots of screaming, so I went into the house through the back door to see what was happening. They were all there. I wasn't sorry. He deserved it. Everybody hated him.

Dwight ("Ike") Dubois, 60

Lydia Tifton's brother.
Was Olympic rifle shooting champion.
Drinks heavily.
Drives a Cadillac.
Doesn't work—spends time hunting and fishing.
Was manager of Pontchartrain Land Development Corporation, one of Tifton's companies.
Went to prison for two years when the company collapsed with debts of over $2 million after a big land scandal.
Has lived in the Tifton mansion since getting out of prison.

Dwight Dubois's statement

I was out by the pond, fishing in my usual spot. When I heard the shots, I hurried through the trees toward the house. I saw Benson running across the lawn toward the study. When I got there, everybody was in the room, except Cajun, the chauffer. Poor old Johnny was dead. I know a dead man when I see one. After all, I was in the army during the war.

Harold Benson, 65

Butler. Has worked for the Tifton family for nearly forty years.
Retires in two months.
Likes good wine and good food.
Takes Lydia Tifton out every day in her wheelchair.
Knows everything about the family.
Had long argument with old man Tifton in the morning.
Knows Ruth Ellen's mother very well.
Introduced Ruth Ellen to old man Tifton.

Benson's statement

I was about to take my afternoon walk. The doctor told me to walk twice a day for my heart. Anyway, I had just come out of the back door, and I was walking around the corner of the house when I heard shooting. I ran across the lawn to the French windows. I saw Mr. John's body and Miss Ruth Ellen in the doorway.

Part 2

Chief of Detectives Tony Damato is in charge of the case. Detective Sergeant Novak is his assistant. They're in the Tifton study.

Damato: Where is everybody?

Novak: They're all in the living room. Reyes is with them. What do you think?

Damato: It could have been any of them, couldn't it? We don't know what skeletons are in the closet! It might even have been all of them. Nobody seems very sad.

Novak: Yeah. Tifton wasn't exactly popular around here. Nobody liked him. It could have been an outsider.

Damato: No, Novak. It must have been one of them. Let's look at the evidence.

Novak: It seems to me that everybody has a motive, and nobody has an alibi. They all say they were alone when it happened.

Damato: Yes, and there are no fingerprints on the gun.

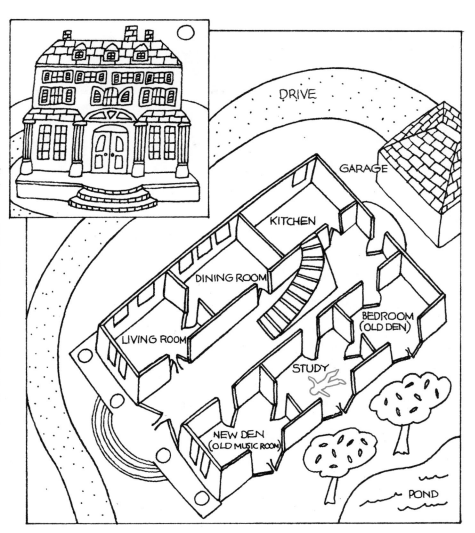

Lydia Tifton?

Novak: It couldn't have been her.

Damato: Why not?

Novak: Well, she's in a wheelchair. She can't move very fast. Anyway, they've been married for thirty-five years. It just couldn't have been her.

Damato: Most murders are committed by someone in the family, Novak, and that door goes into her room.

Novak: Right, but it was locked.

Damato: Doors have keys.

Novak: But why would she want to kill him?

Damato: Ruth Ellen Potts is a very attractive young woman. We don't know what was going on. The old woman might have been jealous.

Novak: But he was over sixty! He was old enough to be her father.

Damato: Hmm . . . yes, but he was a good-looking man—and very rich and powerful.

Dwight Dubois?

Damato: What about Dubois, Novak? He's a weird guy.

Novak: I've been thinking about that. It couldn't have been him.

Damato: Why not?

Novak: Why would he need to shoot five times? He was a champion marksman. He could have killed him with one shot.

Damato: Maybe he did, Novak, maybe he did.

Novak: I don't follow.

Damato: There are a lot of things you don't follow, Novak. Maybe he's smarter than he looks.

Novak: But there's no motive.

Damato: There might have been. I mean there was the scandal with that land development company.

Novak: But he was down by the pond.

Damato: He might have been. He's a champion marksman. He could have shot him from the trees and thrown the gun into the room.

Novak: Oh, yeah. Do you really think so?

Damato: I don't know. It's just a theory.

Look at this:

Could	it have been	him? her? them?

It	must could(n't) may (not) might (not)	have been	him. her. them.

Could	he she they	have	shot him? killed him? been the one(s)?

He She They	must could(n't) may (not) might (not)	have	shot him. killed him. been the one.

Exercise

Discuss each character. Make a list of sentences about all six suspects. Who do you think did it? How? Why?

CONSUMER PROTECTION

Complaining about a defective product or about bad service is never easy. Most people don't like making scenes. However, when you buy consumer products, it is important to know your rights. In the United States, certain rights may be a little different from one state to another, but you have basic rights under federal law in any part of the country. The following information is taken from a pamphlet produced by the Federal Trade Commission. It gives advice to consumers.

Warranties: There Ought To Be a Law…

The Magnusson-Moss Warranty Act helps you *before* you buy by letting you see the warranties. Warranties on consumer products costing more than $15 must be available for you to look at before you buy so you can make comparisons and get the best warranty. And, the Warranty Act helps you *after* you buy by making it easier for you to force companies to keep their warranty promises.

Some Basic Points
Under the Warranty Act, all warranties must be easy to read and understand. All the conditions must be spelled out in writing. Be careful with spoken explanations. What the sales clerk says about the warranty is one thing; what's written may be another.
Note: The law doesn't require warranties except on certain products. If you buy a product "as is," you will have to pay for any repairs.

What Kinds of Warranties Are There?

Written Warranties.
There are two kinds of written warranties: Full and Limited.
A Full Warranty means all this:
- A defective product will be fixed or replaced free.
- It will be fixed within a reasonable time.
- You will not have to do anything unreasonable to get warranty service (such as ship a piano to the factory).
- The warranty is good for the whole warranty period, even for a second or third owner.
- If the product can't be fixed or hasn't been fixed after a reasonable number of tries, you get your choice of a new one or your money back.

But there is one important thing the word "Full" doesn't promise. A Full Warranty doesn't have to cover the whole product. It might cover only part of the product, like the picture tube of a TV. Or it might leave out some parts, like the tires on a car. Always check what parts the warranty covers.

A Limited Warranty gives you less than what a Full Warranty gives. "Limited" means "be careful — something's missing." For example a Limited Warranty might:
- Cover only parts, not labor.
- Allow a partial refund or credit according to the time that has passed since you bought the product.
- Require you to return a heavy product to the store for service.
- Cover only the original owner.
- Charge for handling.

A product can carry more than one written warranty. For example, it can have a Full Warranty on part of the product and a Limited Warranty on the rest.

Implied Warranties
These are rights under state law, not given by the company. All states have them. The most common implied warranty is the "warranty of merchantability." This means that the seller promises that the product you buy is fit for the ordinary uses of the product. For example, a reclining chair must recline; a toaster must toast. If it doesn't, you have a legal right to get your money back. Another implied warranty is the "warranty of fitness for a particular purpose." If a seller tells you that a product can be used for a special purpose, this advice is a warranty. For example, a seller who suggests a certain sleeping bag for zero-degree weather is promising that the sleeping bag will be suitable for zero degrees.

Implied warranties come automatically with every sale. If you get a written warranty, you get the implied warranties too.

Other warranties. Spoken promises and advertising can be warranties too. You have a legal right to get what the company promises.

If The Problem Isn't Solved
Your warranty rights don't run out at the end of the warranty period for problems you complained about during the warranty period. The company must still take care of those problems, no matter how long it takes.

How You Can Use Warranties
Read warranties before you buy to get the best deal. Sometimes it's better to pay more for a product with a better warranty. The extra money is like insurance, but remember that a warranty is only as good as the company that stands behind it. A 20-year warranty by a fly-by-night company might not be a help when you need it.

Read the warranty when a problem comes up. The warranty is a contract that spells out your rights. The company must do what it promises. Keep your receipt with your warranty. You might need it to prove the date you bought the product or that you were the original owner.

The Federal Trade Commission enforces the Warranty Act. To report violations of the law, write to the FTC, Warranties, Washington, DC 20580, or contact FTC Regional Offices in Atlanta, Boston, Chicago, Cleveland, Dallas, Denver, Los Angeles, San Francisco, and Seattle.

MAKING A COMPLAINT

174 Logan Drive
San Diego, CA 92013
May 22, 1984

Customer Service Dept.
Peers Lowbuck Co.
Chicago, IL 60606

Dear Sir or Madam:

Last week I bought a pocket calculator at your store in Anaheim, California. It seemed to work in the store. When I got home, I found it was defective. It performs arithmetic functions perfectly well, but the memory function does not operate. I took it back to your store in San Diego, but they refused to exchange it. They said that I would have to return it to the store where I bought it. This is impossible because I do not live in Anaheim. Enclosed please find the calculator along with the receipt, showing the price and date of purchase, and your guarantee.

Thank you for your attention to this matter.

Sincerely,

Gail Yamamura

(Mrs.) Gail Yamamura

Customer: Good morning. I'd like to speak to the manager.

Manager: I am the manager, sir. How can I help you?

Customer: Oh, yes. It's this radio. It doesn't work.

Manager: Hmm . . . did you buy it here?

Customer: Pardon me? Of course I bought it here. Look, you turn it on and nothing happens.

Manager: May I see your receipt?

Customer: Receipt? I don't have one.

Manager: You must have gotten a receipt when you bought it.

Customer: I probably did. I must have thrown it away.

Manager: Uh huh. Well, do you have any other proof of purchase—the guarantee, for example?

Customer: No. It must have been in the box. I threw that away too.

Manager: Oh dear. You really ought to have kept it. We need to know the exact date of purchase.

Customer: What? I only bought it yes-terday! That young man over there waited on me. Oh, I paid by credit card. I have my copy here.

Manager: Oh. All right then. Did you test the radio before you left the store?

Customer: Test it? No, it was in the original box. I expected it to work. It wasn't some cheap radio; it's a good brand.

Manager: You should have tested it.

Customer: Come on! Stop telling me what I should have done, and do something! Either give me my money back or give me another radio.

Manager: There's no need to get impatient, sir. Let me look at it. Hmm . . . you see this little switch in the back?

Customer: Yes.

Manager: It's on "AC" and it should be on "DC." You really should have read the instructions.

Customer: Oh!

Exercise

Write a letter of complaint. You bought the clock at a Goodworth store on Main Street in your town last week. It said "blue" on the box, but it was pink. The alarm doesn't seem to work. You paid cash, and you didn't keep the receipt.

Unit 27

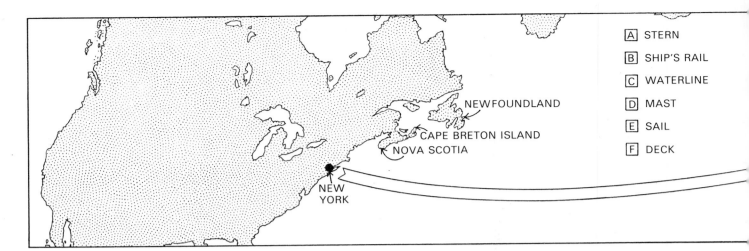

A STERN
B SHIP'S RAIL
C WATERLINE
D MAST
E SAIL
F DECK

NEWFOUNDLAND
CAPE BRETON ISLAND
NOVA SCOTIA
NEW YORK

THE "MARY CELESTE"

The *Mary Celeste* was built in 1861 in Nova Scotia, Canada, as a cargo-carrying sailing ship. When it was launched, it was given the name *Amazon*. It was not a lucky ship. The first captain died a few days after it was registered, and on its first voyage in 1862 it was badly damaged in a collision. While it was being repaired in port, it caught fire. In 1863 it crossed the Atlantic for the first time, and in the English Channel it collided with another ship which sank. The *Amazon* was badly damaged itself. Four years later, in 1867, it ran aground on Cape Breton Island, off the Canadian coast. The ship was almost completely wrecked and had to be rebuilt. It was then sold and the name was changed to the *Mary Celeste*. Sailors are very superstitious and dislike sailing on ships which have been unlucky or which have changed their names. Many sailors refused to sail on the *Mary Celeste*.

On November 5, 1872, the *Mary Celeste* left New York, carrying a cargo of industrial alcohol to Genoa in Italy. There were eleven people on board: Captain Briggs, his wife and two-year-old daughter, and a crew of eight. Briggs was an experienced captain and a very religious man. In his cabin there was a harmonium, which was used for playing hymns.

A month later the *Mary Celeste* was seen by another ship, the *Dei Gratia,* about halfway between the Azores and the Portuguese coast. Captain Moorhouse of the *Dei Gratia,* a friend of Captain Briggs, noticed that the ship was sailing strangely. When the *Mary Celeste* did not answer his signal, he decided to investigate. He sent a small boat to find out what was wrong.

The *Mary Celeste* was completely deserted.
- The only lifeboat was missing.
- All the sails were up and in good condition.
- All the cargo was there.
- The ship had obviously been through storms. The glass cover on the compass was broken.
- The windows of the deck cabins had been covered with wooden planks.
- There was 3 feet of water in the cargo hold, which was not enough to be dangerous.
- The water pumps were working perfectly.
- There was enough food for six months and plenty of fresh water.
- All the crew's personal possessions (clothes, boots, pipes and tobacco, etc.) were on board.
- There were toys on the captain's bed.
- There was food and drink on the cabin table.
- Only the navigation instruments and ship's papers were missing.
- The last entry in the ship's log book had been made eleven days earlier, about 600 miles west, but the ship had continued in a straight line.
- The forehatch was found open.

- There were two deep marks on the bow, near the waterline.
- There was a deep cut on the ship's rail, made by an axe.
- There were old brown bloodstains on the deck and on the captain's sword, which was in the cabin.

Captain Moorhouse put some sailors on the *Mary Celeste* who sailed it to Portugal. There was a long official investigation, but the story of what had happened on the ship, and what had happened to the crew, still remains a mystery. Captain Moorhouse and his crew were given the salvage money for bringing the ship to port. Many explanations have been suggested, but none of them have ever been proved.

Exercise
Find words which mean:
1. All the people working on a ship
2. The official, daily, written record of a ship's voyage
3. A religious song
4. Put a boat into the water
5. An instrument that shows the position of "north"
6. A musical instrument, like a small organ
7. A long, thin, narrow, flat piece of wood
8. Payment given to those who save other's property at sea
9. Goods carried on a ship
10. A machine for forcing water into or out of something

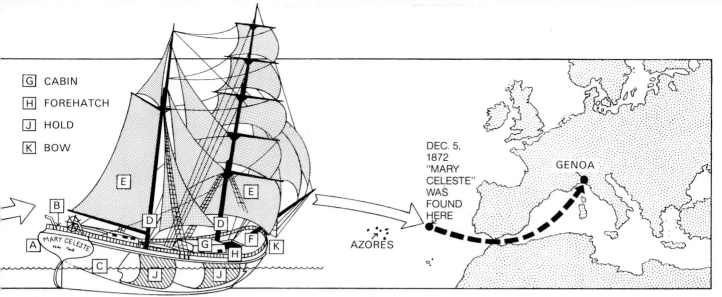

G CABIN
H FOREHATCH
J HOLD
K BOW

DEC. 5, 1872 "MARY CELESTE" WAS FOUND HERE

GENOA

AZORES

What do you think happened?

Sarah: I don't know what happened, but it must have happened suddenly.

Mark: Why do you think that?

Sarah: Think about it. There were toys on the captain's bed, weren't there? The child must have been playing, and they must have interrupted her suddenly.

Mark: Yes, that's true. And the food was on the table. They must have been eating or getting ready to eat.

Sarah: I'll tell you my theory. The lifeboat was missing, right? They could have been practicing their emergency drill. They must have gotten into the boat and launched it.

Mark: All right, but what happened to the boat?

Sarah: Well, they may have been rowing the lifeboat around the ship, and there must have been a gust of wind; then the ship could have moved forward and run down the lifeboat. That explains the marks on the bow.

Mark: Come on. They couldn't have all been sitting in the lifeboat. What about the captain? He should have been steering the ship!

Sarah: Well, he might have been watching the drill and jumped in to save the others.

Some possible explanations of why the crew abandoned the ship.

Amazingly, all of these have been suggested at some time:

1. There was water in the hold. The crew panicked and abandoned the ship because they thought it was going to sink. (Why? The captain was very experienced, and the ship was in good condition. The water pumps were working.)

2. The child fell into the sea. The mother jumped in to save her. They launched a lifeboat to rescue her. (All of them? Why?)

3. One of the barrels of alcohol was damaged. Perhaps there was a small explosion. The hatch cover was off, either because of the explosion or to let the gas escape. They thought all of the cargo might explode. (But there is not much evidence of an explosion.)

4. The last log entry was 600 miles west, near Santa Maria Island. Maybe the ship was in danger of running aground on the island. The crew left the ship in a storm. (How did the ship continue in a straight line for eleven days?)

5. There was no wind, so they got into the lifeboat to tow the ship. The rope broke. (Why were the woman and the child in the lifeboat? Surely the ship was too heavy.)

6. They saw an island which was not on the map and went to investigate. (All of them?)

7. A member of the crew had a terrible, infectious disease. The others left to escape from it. The one with the disease killed himself.

What about the lifeboat?

If the crew left the ship by lifeboat, what happened to them?

1. It could have sunk in a storm.

2. The ship itself could have run down the lifeboat.

3. It could have drifted away, and all of them could have died of hunger and thirst.

4. They might have reached land. They were robbed and killed there.

5. A whale or sharks might even have overturned the boat.

One, or all of them, went crazy.

1. They drank some of the industrial alcohol. There was a fight. Some were killed; the others left. (But industrial alcohol is very poisonous.)

2. The cook was crazy and poisoned everybody. Then he killed himself after throwing the bodies into the sea.

3. The captain had an attack of religious mania, killed everybody, then himself.

4. There was a fungus called "ergot" in the bread. This is a fungus which can grow on rye bread. It is very similar to the drug LSD. Whole villages had been poisoned in this way in medieval Europe.

Crime.

1. The *Dei Gratia* attacked the *Mary Celeste* and killed everybody.

2. Pirates attacked and killed them.

3. There was a mutiny (a revolt against the captain of a ship). Two of the members of the crew were criminals. There was a fight. Some were killed. The others left.

4. Mrs. Briggs fell in love with a crew member. Again there was a fight.

5. The crew of the *Mary Celeste* attacked and robbed another ship and left on the other ship with its cargo. (Which other ship? There are no records.)

6. They found an abandoned ship with a valuable cargo and stole it.

7. Captain Briggs and Captain Moorhouse planned everything together for the salvage money. The ship was never abandoned. None of the story was true.

Outside forces.

1. A spaceship from another planet took everybody away.

2. A giant wave or a tornado knocked them all from the deck.

3. A sea monster (a giant octopus or sea serpent) attacked the ship.

4. Men living below the sea attacked the ship when it passed over the old site of Atlantis.

Unit 29

SPECULATION

1△

Look at this:

He	must	be	crazy.
She	could	have been	at home.
They	may		
It	might	be doing	something.
	can't	have done	
	couldn't	have been doing	

Make as many sentences as possible about each of the pictures.

2△

3△

4△

Unit 30

5△
Richard and Sally Greenhill

6△
Image Bank

7△
John P. Cavanagh/Archive

8△

9△
Will McIntyre/Photo Researchers
New York Daily News

Colorific

11△
10
△
John Hillelson Agency, Ltd.
12△
Gerard Rancinan/Sygma

Unit 30

APOLOGIES

G: Hey, you!
H: Are you talking to me?
G: Yes, you. What do you think you're doing?
H: Huh? I'm just waiting for the bus.
G: Can't you see there's a line?
H: Oh, there is? I'm sorry. I didn't mean to butt in. I didn't realize there was a line.

C: Excuse me. Would you mind putting out your cigarette?
D: I beg your pardon?
C: This is the no-smoking section.
D: It is? I asked for the smoking section.
C: The smoking section is back there.
D: Oh, you're right. I'm awfully sorry.

A: Hello?
B: Hi, Rafael. This is Alex.
A: Oh. Hi. Did you get home all right?
B: Yeah, thanks, but I wanted to apologize for last night.
A: Don't worry about it.
B: But your carpet! It must be ruined. It was so dumb of me to put my coffee on the floor.
A: Come on, Alex, forget it.
B: But it must have made a really ugly stain.
A: Look, it's nothing. I was upset at first, but it doesn't look so bad this morning.
B: Anyway, I want to pay for the cleaning.
A: Listen, Alex, it's no big deal. Accidents happen—at parties especially. I don't want to hear another word about it, O.K.?
B: Well, if you say so, but I really am sorry.
A: See you on Monday. Bye now.

E: Oh! Good morning, Mary Ann.
F: Good afternoon, Sharon. Late again, I see.
E: (Sigh) Yes. I'm sorry. I couldn't find a parking place.
F: Maybe you should have left home earlier.
E: Yes, I know. It won't happen again, Mary Ann.
F: It'd better not, Sharon. This is the third time this week.

I: Are you all right?
J: Yes, I'm O.K., but what about my car?
I: There doesn't seem to be too much damage.
J: Let me see ... look at that! This is a brand new car! You shouldn't have been going so fast.
I: Well, it wasn't my fault.
J: It wasn't your fault?! What do you mean, it wasn't your fault? I had the right of way.
I: As a matter of fact you didn't. You shouldn't have come out like that.
J: Why not? There's no sign.
I: Then what's that?
J: Oh. A stop sign. I must have missed it.
I: Well, you should have been more careful. You could have gotten us all killed.
J: Yes, I see that now. I'm sorry. What else can I say?
I: Just thank God nobody's hurt. Here come the police. You'd better explain it to them.

Unit 31

THEY DIDN'T STOP TO TELL ME!

Police examine abandoned trucks in Bedford.

TRUCK HIJACKED IN BEDFORD
$100,000 Cargo Stolen

A truck carrying television sets, video recorders, microwave ovens, radios, business machines, and vacuum cleaners valued at over $100,000 was hijacked yesterday morning. The truck belonged to the Ruby Star Company, and the driver, Nicolas Estrella, was making deliveries to customers in the Bedford section.

This is the thirty-seventh truck hijacking in the first five months of this year. Over the last four years there have been 386 hijackings in the metropolitan area. The cargoes have ranged from 200,000 labels for Sergio Potentes jeans to Louise Nettlesome sculptures, from meat and cheese to champagne.

Drivers have been warned to be careful about locking their doors and have been warned not to pick up hitchhikers. Some insurance investigators believe that as many as one-third of these cases are not hijackings at all. They believe that dishonest drivers steal their own cargoes. The police point to the other culprits in these cases of urban thievery.

"The retail store owners who buy stolen goods make very big profits. They are the real criminals," said Police Capt. Mel Torino. "The hijackers steal because they can sell."

The hijackers seem to be both well-organized and well-informed. They concentrate on trucks carrying cargoes that can be sold quickly for cash. (continued on page A6)

Police Captain Mel Torino is questioning Nicolas Estrella, the driver of the hijacked Ruby Star truck.

Captain: Have a seat, Mr. Estrella. Cigarette?

Mr. Estrella: No, thanks, Captain. I'm trying to stop smoking.

Captain: Let's start at the beginning again. How did you lose your truck?

Mr. Estrella: You know the story already.

Captain: I'm sorry to do this, but I'm kind of slow. Tell me again.

Mr. Estrella: O.K. I was making deliveries in Bedford. The truck was loaded with TVs and radios.

Captain: Uh huh. So you drove to the Bedford section from the Ruby Star warehouse.

Mr. Estrella: Right. About 10 o'clock I made a delivery on Boyle Street. I'd finished and I was driving up Boyle when I saw a coffee shop.

Captain: So you decided to stop.

Mr. Estrella: That's right. I stopped to get a cup of coffee to go.

Captain: Go on.

Mr. Estrella: It didn't take me more than three minutes. I started walking back to the truck and . . .

Captain: Did you see anybody near the truck?

Mr. Estrella: No, nobody. So anyway, I decided to make a phone call.

Captain: A phone call?

Mr. Estrella: You can check that. I passed a magazine stand and I stopped to get change.

Captain: O.K. Then what?

Mr. Estrella: Well, I was talking to my wife when I saw the truck going down the street. I couldn't believe my eyes. I dropped the phone and ran down the street. But they were moving fast. I couldn't catch up.

Captain: Did you remember to lock the cab door?

Mr. Estrella: Yes, I always remember to lock it! I'm not that stupid!

Captain: O.K., O.K., take it easy. Can you actually remember locking it this time?

Mr. Estrella: Yes, definitely.

Captain: How can you be so sure?

Mr. Estrella: Well, I remember putting the key in the lock. It was all wet and dirty. It was raining, and I had dropped it in a puddle.

Captain: What about the door on the other side. Did you remember to check it?

Mr. Estrella: I don't actually remember checking it. But it's always locked, and I never use it.

Captain: But you don't remember checking it?

Mr. Estrella: No, not really. Maybe I forgot to check it.

Captain: So it could have been open.

Mr. Estrella: Yes, I guess so. But I'd bet anything it wasn't.

Captain: So what's your theory?

Mr. Estrella: They must have had keys. They started the engine, didn't they?

Captain: How did they get the keys?

Mr. Estrella: Don't ask me. I have no idea. They didn't stop to tell me!

Look at this:

He was driving. He stopped. He got some coffee.

A. *What did he stop doing? He stopped driving.*
B. *What did he stop to do? He stopped to get some coffee.*

Exercise 1
Ask two questions and give answers.
1. He was driving. He stopped. He bought some gas.
2. He was watching the truck. He stopped. He made a phone call.
3. He was talking to his wife. He stopped. He ran down the street.

Look at this:

I drove a car for the first time when I was sixteen. I was so nervous but so happy that day! *I remember driving a car for the first time.*

I was going to mail this letter. I still have it. *I didn't remember to mail it.* *I forgot to mail it.*

Exercise 2
Make sentences.
1. I should have turned off the light. It's still on.
2. I read about the crime in the newspaper. I can remember it clearly.
3. There's a movie on TV tonight. I saw it at a theater ten years ago.
4. They ought to have done their homework. The teacher's very upset.

Unit 32

JOHN LENNON 1940-1980

John Lennon was murdered just before 11 p.m. on December 8, 1980, outside the Dakota, an apartment building where he lived in New York City. He had just gotten out of a car and was walking to the entrance when a voice called, "Mr. Lennon." Lennon turned and was shot five times. The killer threw his gun down and stood there smiling. "Do you know what you just did?" shouted the doorman. "I just shot John Lennon," the killer replied. Lennon was rushed to the hospital in a police car, but it was too late. The killer was 25 year-old Mark Chapman from Hawaii. Earlier the same evening he had asked Lennon for his autograph. In fact, he had been hanging around outside the apartment building for several days. Chapman was a fan of Lennon and had tried to imitate him in many ways. It is said that he even believed that he was John Lennon.

Biographical Notes

1940 Born in Liverpool, England.
1942 Lennon family deserted by father. Mother leaves. John brought up by aunt.
1956 Forms rock band at school.
1957 Student at Liverpool College of Art.
1958 Mother killed in car accident.
1960 Goes professional as one of "The Beatles" (Lennon, McCartney, Harrison, Best, Sutcliffe). Plays in Hamburg, Germany.
1961 Plays in Hamburg and Liverpool. Sutcliffe (Lennon's best friend) dies of brain tumor. Brian Epstein begins to manage the Beatles.
1962 Ringo Starr replaces Pete Best as Beatles drummer. Married Cynthia Powell, an art student. Beatles' first record "Love Me Do." First TV appearance.

1963 Three records Number 1 in British Top 20. Incredible popularity. Son Julian born.
1964 First hit record in U.S. "I Want to Hold Your Hand." Two U.S. tours. In April, Beatles' records Number 1, 2, 3, 4, and 5 in U.S. Top 20. First movie *A Hard Day's Night*. First book.
1965 *Help!* Beatles' second movie. Beatlemania at its height. U.S. tour. Huge audiences in sports stadiums. Beatles receive MBE (special honorary award) from Queen Elizabeth.

1966 Lennon in movie *How I Won the War*—not a musical. Meets Yoko Ono, Japanese avant-garde artist.
1967 "Sergeant Pepper"—Beatles' most famous album. All the Beatles interested in meditation. Manager Brian Epstein found dead from overdose of sleeping pills.
1968 In India with Beatles for meditation. Beatles' company, Apple, founded. Lennon art exhibit "You Are Here." Lennon divorced by wife.
1969 Beatles' movie *Let It Be*. Rumors of quarrels about money. Talk of Beatles breaking up. Beatles' last public performance on roof of Apple Building. Lennon and Yoko marry. He 29, she 36. Lennon still recording with Beatles but some work solo.

1970 McCartney leaves Beatles. Others start solo careers.
1971 Lennon's album "Imagine"—most successful album. Lennon and Yoko Ono in New York one-room studio apartment.
1972 Charity concerts.
1973 Lennon and Yoko Ono separate. Lennon in Los Angeles. Lennon ordered to leave U.S.—protests and appeals.
1974 Drinking problems—still fighting deportation.
1975 Lennon and Yoko Ono together again in New York. Permission to stay in U.S. Son Sean born October 9 (Lennon's birthday).
1976 Retires from public life. Extensive travel. Business affairs managed by Yoko Ono.
1976 Full-time father. Very close relationship with son. Owns seven apartments in same building—one for cold storage of fur coats.
1980 First record in six years. Album "Double Fantasy." Single "Starting Over." Good reviews from critics. Many said it was "a new beginning." Dec. 8 Lennon murdered. Massive media coverage. TV and radio programs interrupted to give news. Record companies on overtime to meet demand for records.
1981 Three records in Top 20 charts: "(Just Like) Starting Over," "Imagine," and "Woman."
1984 Lennon's last album, "Milk and Honey" released. "Nobody Told Me" reaches Top 20.

n't $1,240 make Christmas merry?
for your lucky TV Prevue number on page 5

Sun-Times
Chicago, Tuesday, December 9, 1980
25¢ city and suburbs, 30¢ elsewhere
★★★★★ Turf Final

Lennon slain
shot in Manhattan

NEWS
WEDNESDAY, DECEMBER 9, 1980
Rain. High 45 to 50. Details p. 68

LENNON
HERE
West Side

robe finds
sabotage at
n Station
Page 3

KIDNAPPED

Dr. Pamela Crane-Newton and Dr. Daniel Newton work at the same hospital in Phoenix, Arizona. Pamela is a cardiologist, and Daniel is a neurosurgeon. They usually come home together at six and have dinner with their daughter, Caroline. Tonight the house was dark when they arrived, and there was no sign of Caroline. On the floor, near the door, there was a note. Pamela picked it up, read it, and tears came to her eyes.

Daniel: Pamela, what's wrong? Is it from Caroline?

Pamela: No ... yes ... no. She ... (sob) ... She's been kidnapped!

Daniel: Kidnapped! Let me see that ... Oh, no! Oh, my God! (Sob) No, no, no!

Pamela: I'll call the police.

Daniel: No, Pamela! Don't touch the phone!

Pamela: Oh yes, the note says not to. Let's read it again—carefully.

Daniel: A million dollars!

Pamela: How long will it take us to get that much cash together?

Daniel: I don't know. Maybe we should call the police.

Pamela: No, Daniel. If the kidnappers find out, they'll kill her.

Daniel: But we'll have to borrow the money. If we don't tell the police, the bank won't let us have it.

Pamela: But remember what the note says. Unless we do exactly as they say, we may never see her again.

Daniel: Hello?

Voice: Did you find our note?

Daniel: Yes. We found it.

Voice: Have you told the police?

Daniel: No, we ... No, not yet.

Voice: You'd better not. When can you get the money?

Daniel: We need a few days.

Voice: You have one day.

Daniel: How do we know that Caroline is still alive?

Voice: You don't. You'll have to trust us. Get the money by tomorrow night. You'll hear from us again.

Daniel: If you harm a hair on her head, I'll ... I'll ...

> WE have your daughter
> She is safe and sound
> We WANT $1,000,000
> IF YOU give us the money
> she will be OK Don't call
> the police or we'll kill her
> IF you try to contact them WE'LL know
> If you don't follow our
> instructions your Daughter will die
> Unless you PAY up you'll never
> see HER again

Exercise 1

1. If you were in Daniel and Pamela's place, would you call the police?
2. If you were in the kidnappers' place, how would you arrange to get the money?
3. If you were Daniel and Pamela, what would you do?
4. If you were the police, what would you do?

Exercise 2

A: *Give me the money!*
B: *Why should I?*
A: *If you don't give me the money, I'll kill you.*
B: *What?! You're crazy!*
A: *Maybe, but unless you give me the money, I'll kill you.*

Now look at the pictures, and make similar conversations.

STOP SMOKING OR YOU WON'T LIVE VERY LONG.

MARRY ME OR I'LL KILL MYSELF.

Exercise 3

Look at Exercise 2.
What would you do in the three situations?
If I were him, I'd give him the money.
If I were him, I'd hide under the counter.
If I were him, I'd pull the alarm.

Unit 34

HAVE YOU SEEN THIS AD?

Mike: Wendy, have you seen this ad?
Wendy: Yeah. It looks great, doesn't it? I called them an hour ago. They'll call back if they want me.
Mike: Oh, they'll want you for sure. I mean you have beautiful hair.
Wendy: I hope so. If I go, I'll get a new hairdo—and have a lot of fun too.

Louis: Pablo, look at this.
Pablo: Oh yeah, I've seen it. I'm going to call tomorrow.
Louis: It sounds very exciting, and you have a decent car.
Pablo: Uh huh. There are some disadvantages.
Louis: Every job has disadvantages, but you're always complaining about the job you have now.
Pablo: Oh, I don't know. I'm willing to try it. But I won't take it if they don't pay the phone bill!

Roger: Tina, what do you think of this ad?
Tina: Didn't I tell you? It was in last Sunday's paper too. I called. I have an interview tomorrow.
Roger: Do you think you'll get it?
Tina: They seemed very interested on the phone. I think they'll offer me the job.
Roger: So you're going to Mandanga!
Tina: I didn't say that. I won't take the job unless they give me a round trip ticket. It'll be hard work, and I won't go unless they offer me a good salary.

Sandy: Hey, Bill, look at this ad.
Bill: Hmm . . . It looks like fun. Why don't you call them up?
Sandy: I'd love to, but it's a waste of time. My hair's just too short.
Bill: Well, I like it the way it is. Anyway, you don't know what they might do. Hair standing up in spikes is really fashionable now.
Sandy: Oh, Bill, that wouldn't bother me. If I had longer hair, I'd call them up. Actually, *your* hair is pretty long now . . .

Kathy: Lynn, did you see this?
Lynn: Yeah. You aren't interested, are you?
Kathy: What! Me? I wasn't born yesterday! There are too many things wrong with it.
Lynn: Like what?
Kathy: I wouldn't take a job like that! You wouldn't have any security. You wouldn't earn anything if you didn't work all day long every day. And I wouldn't take a job in sales if they didn't provide the car.
Lynn: Yeah, and look at the address—some hotel. I'd never work for a company if they didn't even have an office.

Kitty: There's a job in Mandanga in the paper.
Terry: Yeah, I know. I wouldn't dream of taking it.
Kitty: Why not? You've been looking for a job in a foreign country.
Terry: It's slave labor, isn't it? One night off a week.
Kitty: But the money might be good.
Terry: Hmph! I wouldn't take it unless they paid me a really good salary with a longer vacation and more free time. And I certainly wouldn't go off to a place like Mandanga unless my ticket was round trip!

Exercise
Could you ever kill a person?
Not unless they tried to kill me.
I wouldn't kill anybody unless they tried to kill me.
What about these things?
Would you ever steal food/rob a bank/hit someone/eat a dog or cat/ jump from a high building/take your clothes off in the street/go sky diving (with a parachute)/have a heart transplant?

Look at this:

I'm interested. I've applied.	I'm not interested. I haven't applied.
I'll accept the job if they offer enough money.	I'd apply if they offered more money.
I won't accept the job if they don't pay more.	I wouldn't accept the job if they didn't offer enough.
I won't accept the job unless they pay more.	I wouldn't accept the job unless they offered more.

"Good evening. This is Ted Cooper with MBS Late Night Report. Tonight, in our first segment, we're looking again at the problem of the world's limited energy resources. Nobody knows exactly how much fuel is left, but pessimistic forecasts say that there is only enough coal for 450 years and enough natural gas for 50 years and that oil might run out in 30 years. Obviously we have to do something, and we have to do it soon. Debate continues about the use of nuclear power to solve this crisis. First, we go by satellite to the studios of WLNN in Boston to hear from Professor William White of the New England Institute of Technology."

"Well, Mr. Cooper, we are in a long-range energy crisis. With lower oil prices people have forgotten that, as you said, fossil fuels—coal, oil and gas—are running out. The tragedy is that fossil fuels are far too valuable to waste on the production of electricity. Just think of all the things we make from oil! If we don't start conserving these things now, it will be too late. And nuclear power is the only real alternative. We are getting some electricity from nuclear power plants already. If we invest in further research now, we'll be ready to face the future. There's been a lot of protest lately against nuclear power—some people will protest anything—but nuclear power plants are not as dangerous as some people say. It's far more dangerous to work down in a coal mine or on an offshore oil rig. Safety regulations in nuclear power plants are very strict.

"If we spent money on research now, we could develop plants which create their own fuel and burn their own waste. In many parts of the world where there are no fossil fuels, nuclear power is the only alternative. If you accept that we need electricity, then we will need nuclear energy. Just imagine what the world would be like if we didn't have electricity—no heating, no lighting, no industry, no radio or TV. Just think about the ways you use electricity every day. Surely we don't want to go back to the Stone Age. That's what will happen if we turn our backs on nuclear research."

"Thank you, Professor White. Now we join our affiliate KJEM in San Francisco, where Jean Black is waiting to give us the position of CANE, the Campaign Against Nuclear Energy."

"Ted, I must disagree totally with

ENERGY CRISIS

Professor White. Let's look at the facts. First, there is no perfect machine. I mean, why do planes crash? Machines fail. People make mistakes. What would happen if there were a serious nuclear accident? And an accident is inevitable—sooner or later. Huge areas would be evacuated, and they could remain contaminated with radioactivity for years, and not a penny in compensation! No insurance company covers nuclear risks. There are accidents all the time. If the nuclear industry didn't keep them quiet, there would be a public outcry. Radioactivity causes cancer and may affect future generations.

"Next, nuclear waste. There is no technology for absolutely safe disposal. Some of this waste will remain radioactive for thousands of years. Is that what you want to leave to your children? And their children's children?

"Next, terrorism. Terrorists could blackmail the whole country if they captured a reactor. The Savannah River nuclear plant, and Professor White knows this very well, lost (yes, lost!) enough plutonium between 1955 and 1978 to make 18 (18!) atomic

bombs. Where is it? Who has it? I believe that nuclear energy is expensive, dangerous, evil, and most of all, absolutely unnecessary. I think your next guest will be saying more about that."

"Yes, thank you, Ms. Black, you're right. By satellite we now join Dr. Catalina Burgos at WFAM in Chicago. Dr. Burgos is the author of several books on alternative technology."

"Hello, Mr. Cooper. I'd like to begin by agreeing with Jean. We can develop alternative sources of power, and unless we try we'll never succeed. Instead of burning fossil fuels we should be concentrating on more economic uses of electricity, because electricity can be produced from any source of energy. If we didn't waste so much energy, our resources would last longer. You can save more energy by conservation than you can produce for the same money. Unless we do research on solar energy, wind power, wave power, tidal power, hydroelectric projects, etc., our fossil fuels will run out, and we'll all freeze or starve to death. Other countries are spending much more than we do on research, and don't forget that energy from the sun, the waves, and the wind lasts forever. We really won't survive unless we start working on cleaner, safer sources of energy."

"Thank you very much, Dr. Burgos. Our final speaker on the subject of energy is in the studios of WGMT in Washington, D.C. He is Joseph Huang, Under Secretary of Energy. Mr. Huang."

"I've been listening to the other speakers with great interest. By the way, I don't agree with some of the estimates of world energy reserves. More oil and gas is being discovered all the time. If we listened to the pessimists (and there are a lot of them around) none of us would sleep at night. In the short run, we must continue to rely on the fossil fuels—oil, coal, and gas. But we must also look to the future. Our policy must be flexible. Unless we thought new research was necessary, we wouldn't be spending money on it. After all, we wouldn't have a Department of Energy unless most people thought it was important. The big question is where to spend the money—on conservation of present resources or on research into new forms of power. But I'm fairly optimistic. I wouldn't be in this job unless I were an optimist!"

WHAT WOULD YOU HAVE DONE?

THE READER'S PAGE

What would you have done?

Last week we invited you, the readers, to write and tell us about things that had happened to you, or things that you had heard about. We wanted stories where people just didn't know what to do next! Here are the stories that interested us the most!

That's my beer...or was

I was in a bar in a small Western town. I had just been served a glass of beer. Suddenly this huge man — he looked like a boxer — came over, picked up my beer, drank it, banged the glass down on the table, stared at me, and then walked away without saying anything. I suppose I should have said something, but I was scared stiff! I didn't know what to do! What would you have done?
Stanley Wempe • Carbondale, IL

In deep water

I was driving through Oregon on my vacation. It was a very hot day, and I stopped at a small deserted beach. I didn't have my bathing suit with me, but it was early in the morning and there were no people or houses in sight. So I took off my clothes and swam out in the ocean in my underwear. I'm a very strong swimmer. I floated on my back, closed my eyes, and relaxed in the water. When I looked back at the beach, several cars had arrived and there were twenty or thirty people sitting on the sand having a picnic! What would you have done?
Jane Dare • Spokane, WA

That's a no-no

I heard a great story about the Rev. Billy Cracker. He'd gone to

London to speak at a large meeting. Anyway, when he stepped off the plane there were a lot of reporters and TV cameras. The first question one of the reporters asked was, "Do you intend to visit any nightclubs in London?" Rev. Cracker smiled at the reporter. "Are there any nightclubs in London?" he answered innocently. The next morning the headline in one of the London papers was "Cracker's first question on arrival in London — Are there any nightclubs?" How would you have felt?
Rev. Aural Richards • Columbia, SC

Strangers in the night

My story isn't funny at all. It was a very frightening experience. You

see, one night I woke up suddenly. I heard the tinkle of broken glass from downstairs, and I heard the window opening. Then I heard two voices! My wife woke up too. She told me to do something. A couple of days before there had been a report about a burglary in the local paper. The burglars had been interrupted, and they had beaten up the home-owner. They'd nearly killed him. I was trembling with fear. I just didn't know what to do. In the end, I didn't go down, and they stole the sterling silverware we had inherited from my mother. Was I right? What would you have done?
Lorenzo Machado • Abeline, TX

Deep fried

I had parked my car at a local shopping mall, and I was taking a

short cut through the side door of a restaurant. Halfway across the restaurant, I spotted my father eating a hamburger and french fries — he often eats there. I sneaked up behind him, put my hand over his shoulder, took a french fry off the plate, dipped it in catsup and ate it. Then I realized that the man was not my father! I was so embarrassed! I couldn't say a word! What would you have done?
Cheryl Redburn • Minneapolis, MN

Or else

I'd just parked my car on a street near the football stadium in Des Moines. It was ten minutes before the start of the game and I was in a hurry. Two little boys came up to me and said, "Give us $5 and we'll watch your car while you're at the game." I told them to clear out, and one of them looked at me with big, round, innocent eyes and said, "Unless you give us the money, something might happen to your car while you're away. You know, a scratch or a flat tire. Something like that." I was furious! What would you have done?
Helen Furie • Des Moines, IO

Honesty is the best policy

I couldn't believe a story I heard the other day. It seems that a woman had just bought a house in Burlingon, Vermont. She wanted to insulate the roof, so she and her son climbed up into the attic. There, under the hot water tank, was $50,000 in cash! They turned in the money to the police. Would you have reported the find? What would you have done?
Francine Marasco • Waterbury, VT

Look at this:

Would you have said anything?
What would you have done?

I	'd	have	said	something.
	would		done	
	wouldn't			anything.

Exercise 1
Make sentences like this about each of the seven stories.

Exercise 2
Tell the story of an interesting, surprising, or embarrassing experience you have had or heard about.

Unit 37

A BAD DAY AT THE OFFICE

Margot: What was wrong with you this morning?

Tim: Wrong with me? I'm sorry, Margot, I don't know what you mean.

Margot: You walked straight past me. You didn't say a word!

Tim: Really? Where?

Margot: It was just by that newsstand on 34th Street.

Tim: I'm really sorry, Margot. I just didn't see you.

Margot: Come on, Tim. You must have. I was waving!

Tim: No, honestly, I didn't see you. If I had seen you, I would've said hello.

Exercise 1

He didn't see her. He didn't say "hello."

If he had seen her, he would have said "hello."

Do the same:

1. He didn't recognize her. He didn't stop.
2. He didn't notice her. He didn't stop.
3. He didn't see her waving. He didn't wave back.

Peggy: Tim, have you sent that telex to Japan?

Tim: No, I haven't.

Peggy: Why haven't you done it yet? It's urgent.

Tim: Because you didn't ask me to do it.

Peggy: I didn't?

Tim: No, you didn't. If you had asked me, I'd have sent it.

Exercise 2

Have you sent the telex?

If you had asked me, I would have sent it.

Do the same:

1. Have you mailed the letters?
2. Have you photocopied the report?
3. Have you typed the contract?

Connie: Did you see a letter from Brazil on my desk?

Tim: Yes, here it is.

Connie: Oh, good. Where's the envelope?

Tim: I threw it away. Why?

Connie: It had some nice stamps on it. I wanted it for my uncle. He collects stamps.

Tim: Gee, Connie, if I'd known . . .

Connie: It's no big deal.

Tim: I would've kept it if I'd known.

Exercise 3

I didn't keep it.

I would have kept it if I had known.

Do the same:

1. I didn't call.
2. I didn't give it to you.
3. I didn't put it in the drawer.

Tim: What's the matter, Debbie. You don't look well.

Debbie: No. I've had a terrible cold. I've been in bed all weekend, but it's better today.

Tim: Hmm . . . I had a bad cold last week.

Debbie: I know, and you gave it to everyone in the office. I wouldn't have come to work if I'd had a cold like that.

Exercise 4

He had a bad cold, but he came to work.

I wouldn't have come to work if I had had a cold.

Do the same:

1. She had a headache, but she stayed at work.
2. He had a sore throat, but he worked all day.
3. She had a toothache, but she didn't go to the dentist.

Peggy: Tim?

Tim: Yes?

Peggy: Did you type this letter or did Akiko do it?

Tim: I did. Why? Is there something wrong with it?

Peggy: Take a look. This should be $400,000. You typed $40,000.

Tim: Oh yeah. I'm really sorry.

Peggy: And you misspelled the customer's name. It should be "Snelling," not "Smelling."

Tim: (Laugh) Oh, no! Did I put that?

Peggy: It's not funny, Tim. If I hadn't noticed it, we could have lost the order.

Exercise 5

She noticed the error. They didn't lose the order.

If she hadn't noticed the error, they could have lost the order.

Do the same:

1. She noticed the spelling mistake. They didn't upset the customer.
2. She saw it in time. They didn't send the letter.
3. She checked the letter. They didn't mail it.

Henry: Hi, Tim. Did you have a good day today?

Tim: No, not really. I'm glad it's over. Everything went wrong.

Henry: Really?

Tim: Yeah, I made a lot of mistakes in typing, then I forgot to send a telex, and Margot got upset because I ignored her on the street.

Henry: Why was that?

Tim: It was that party last night. If I hadn't gone to bed late, it wouldn't have been such an awful day. I'm going to make it an early night tonight.

Exercise 6

I went to a party./I went to bed late./I forgot to set the alarm./I got up late./I missed the bus./I was late for work./I've had a bad day./I forgot to send a telex./I made a mistake in typing.

If I hadn't gone to the party, none of these things would have happened.

If I hadn't gone to a party, I wouldn't have gone to bed late.

Make eight sentences.

A SATURDAY AFTERNOON

Laura felt slightly uneasy as the guard unlocked the gates and waved her through. The Blitzkopf Clinic was not an ordinary mental institution. It was the most exclusive institution of its type in the country. You had to be not only mentally ill, but also extremely wealthy to be accepted as a patient. She parked her car outside the main entrance of the sterile white main building. She paused on the steps to look at the beautiful flower gardens and surrounding grounds. An old man in a white straw hat was watering the flower bed beside the steps. He smiled at her.

Old man: Good afternoon. Pretty day, isn't it?

Laura: Yes, it certainly is.

Old man: Are you a new patient?

Laura: Oh, I'm not a patient. I'm just here to do some research.

Old man: Will you be staying long?

Laura: I really don't know. I wonder if you could tell me the way to Dr. Blitzkopf's office?

Old man: Certainly. Just go through the main door, turn left, walk down to the end of the hall, and it's the last door on the right.

Laura: Thank you very much.

Dr. Blitzkopf was expecting her. He had been looking forward to meeting his new research assistant. He himself had always been interested in the special problems of long-term patients. Dr. Blitzkopf was very proud of his clinic, and Laura was impressed by the relaxed and informal atmosphere. She spent the mornings interviewing patients and the afternoons in the flower gardens, writing up the results of her research. Some of the patients were withdrawn and depressed; some seemed almost normal. Only one or two had to be kept locked up. She found it hard to believe that all of them had been considered too dangerous to live in normal society. She often saw the old man in the straw hat. He spent most of his time working in the flower gardens, but he always stopped to speak to her. She found out that his name was Edward Beale. He was a gentle and mild-mannered old fellow, with clear, blue, honest eyes, white

hair, and a pinkish complexion. He always looked pleased with life. She became particularly curious about him, but Dr. Blitzkopf had never asked her to interview him, and she wondered why. One night, at dinner, she asked about Mr. Beale.

Dr. Blitzkopf: Ah, yes, Edward. Nice old guy. He's been here longer than anybody.

Laura: What's wrong with him?

Dr. Blitzkopf: Nothing. His family put him here thirty-five years ago. They never come to visit him, but the bills are always paid on time.

Laura: But what had he done?

Dr. Blitzkopf: I'll show you his file. It seems that he burned down his school when he was seventeen. His family tried to keep the incident quiet. Over the next few years there were a number of mysterious fires in his neighborhood, but the family did nothing until he tried to set fire to the family mansion. He was in here the next day. Edward never protested.

Laura: And that was thirty-five years ago!

Dr. Blitzkopf: I'm afraid so. If I'd had my way, I'd have let him out years ago.

Laura: But he couldn't still be dangerous!

Dr. Blitzkopf: No. He's had plenty of opportunities. We even let him smoke. If he'd wanted to start a fire, he could have done it at any time.

Laura was shocked by the story. She became determined to do something about it. She wrote letters to Edward's family, but never received a reply. He had never been officially certified as insane, and legally he could leave at any time. Dr. Blitzkopf was easily persuaded to let her talk to Edward.

Laura: Edward, have you ever thought about leaving this place?

Edward: No. I'm very happy here. This is my home. And anyway, I have nowhere else to go.

Laura: But wouldn't you like to go into town sometimes—to buy your own cigarettes?

Edward: I've never thought about it. I suppose it would be nice. But I wouldn't want to stay away for long. I've spent twenty years working on this garden. I know every flower and tree. What would happen to them if I weren't here?

Laura realized that it would be unkind to make him leave the hospital. However, she found out that the next Saturday was his birthday. She arranged with the staff to give him a party. They wanted it to be a surprise, and Dr. Blitzkopf agreed to let him go out for the afternoon. There was a flower show in town. Edward left at 2 o'clock. He seemed quite excited. They expected him to return about four o'clock. The cook had made a birthday cake, and the staff had decorated the lounge.

Laura was standing in the window when she saw him. He was early. He was walking up the drive toward the house, whistling cheerfully. Behind him, above the trees, thick black columns of smoke were beginning to rise slowly into the clear blue sky.

Can you see yourself riding a cable car in San Francisco, eating fresh crab at Fisherman's Wharf, winning a fortune in the casinos of Las Vegas, and walking with the stars along Hollywood Boulevard? TransAtlantic Airways invites you to spend two unforgettable weeks in California and Nevada and enjoy the glitter and the glamour of the Golden West.

Every city has its own character—San Francisco with the Golden Gate Bridge, Chinatown, Japantown, cable cars climbing up the steep hills, restaurants serving food from every country in the world. You'll go on tours to see the scenery of Monterey and Carmel and the breathtaking views from the Pacific Coast Highway.

Then you join in the excitement of Las Vegas, the gambling capital of the world, set in the Nevada Desert. Las Vegas never sleeps and the entertainment is the finest in the world. And from Las Vegas there's an optional flight over the spectacular Grand Canyon.

Finally you arrive in Los Angeles, home of the movie industry. Sunset Boulevard, Beverly Hills, and Hollywood all wait to welcome you. You'll be able to choose any number of tours—the wonderful world of Disneyland, Universal Studios, or even a shopping spree on Rodeo Drive.

This exciting three-city tour offers you a golden opportunity to experience the special atmosphere of the Golden West.

Matilda is Colombian and married to George Marek, an American teaching in Colombia. They've just returned to Colombia and Matilda is telling her friends about her first trip to the States.

"On the whole I enjoyed it very much, but it was pretty tiring. We went on most of the tours because I didn't want to miss anything. I really felt we needed more time. If I went again, I'd stay longer. I would have spent more time in San Francisco and less time in Los Angeles if I'd known more about the cities. Los Angeles was a little disappointing. We went on a tour of Beverly Hills to see the houses of the stars. But unless you had studied film history, you would never have heard of most of them! Generally speaking, the hotels, food, and service were excellent. And I found Californians particularly friendly. I probably took too much luggage. Clothes in California were so cheap! It would have been a good idea to take along an empty suitcase! If I'd done that, the savings on clothes would almost have paid for half of the air fare! Well, not really . . ."

The Rizzos, a retired couple from Damariscotta, Maine, were on the tour with the Mareks. Jack Rizzo was asked about the trip.

"We'd been looking forward to this trip for years, and it was the vacation of a lifetime. I think we enjoyed Las Vegas the most, but two nights were probably enough! If we'd stayed there much longer, we'd have lost all our money! We saw Dolly Parton at the Desert Inn. I've never seen anything like that place! Disneyland is a 'must' for anyone with children. If only we'd had our grandchildren with us! They would have loved it! We went on some of the tours, and we could have gone on more, but you can't see everything, can you? I didn't think much of the food there, but California wine was a nice surprise. We wouldn't have gone on this trip unless it had been an escorted tour group. We're not as young as we used to be, and we couldn't have done it on our own. Everyone, however, was so helpful to us."

Unit 40

HOLIDAY USA

Fly-Drive means freedom—the freedom of the road to explore this exciting country. Fly-Drive must be the logical way of seeing the Northeast. Get to your first destination by plane and then rent a comfortable car. It allows you the luxury of a flexible schedule—the ideal way of getting the most out of your vacation. We'll make a reservation at a wonderful hotel for your first night and your car will be delivered to you in the morning. Then you are as free as a bird to go and stay anywhere you'd like to. Or you can plan your driving route beforehand and we'll make all of your motel reservations for you in advance. When you prepay, we'll send you all of your motel confirmations, and your room will be waiting for you at each stop.

Boston is the ideal starting point for exploring New England. To the southeast are the rocky cliffs and sandy beaches of beautiful Cape Cod, ideal for swimming, sailing, and fishing. To the north is New Hampshire with its green valleys, lovely steepled churches, and infinite varieties of wildflowers. Drive up into Maine, a land of forests and mountains. Try the lobster in the charming restaurants along the spectacular coastline. Drive west across New York State to Niagara Falls or south through the beautiful rolling hills of Connecticut to a coastline of resort towns and fishing ports.

Luis and Carmen Noguera and their two children flew from Albuquerque, New Mexico to Boston to take the fly-drive vacation. Now Carmen is talking about it.

"We'd never have gone on a fly-drive vacation unless we'd had the kids with us. I think it's the only way to travel with young children. The distances were much greater than we had imagined. If we ever went East on vacation again, we wouldn't try to drive so far. I think we'd cover the longer distances by plane, and then rent a different car in each place. Of course, that gets expensive. We stayed at lovely, quaint country inns, which were perfect for all of us. They weren't too expensive, and the children were always made welcome. In fact, a few of the innkeepers offered to babysit. For us that was marvelous. We wouldn't have been able to leave the children if they hadn't offered. We would never have left them alone for too long, of course, but it was nice for us to get away from them for a few hours. New England was absolutely fantastic and we'd recommend it to anyone, especially in the fall."

Stephanie and Melissa Gold also took the fly-drive vacation from San Diego to visit their grandmother in Hanover, New Hampshire. Melissa spoke about their vacation.

"It was really great. After we visited our grandmother we explored New England. We took turns driving, so the distances didn't seem so long. One night we couldn't find a motel, but it was O.K. because we had rented a 1984 Cutlass Supreme. There was plenty of room to sleep! We bought lots of maple syrup. If we'd bought it in California, it would have cost almost three times as much. We took our vacation in the fall, so the colors of the trees in New England were unbelievable! We wouldn't have chosen this vacation plan unless we'd liked driving. You spend a lot of time in the car. We plan to go to the East Coast again next year, but we'll visit our other grandmother in Miami, if we can afford it."

Unit 40

APPENDIX

Material recorded on cassette but not included in the text of the units is printed below.

Unit 1

1. Streamline Air Flight 604 departing at 2:45 for Kennedy Airport in New York City is now boarding at Gate 3. Passengers with tickets on Streamline 604 at 2:45 to New York Kennedy please check in at Gate 3.

2. This is the last call for Peoplexpress Flight 373 departing at 2:30 for Houston. Passengers on Peoplexpress 373 at 2:30 to Houston should board now at Gate 1.

3. Continental Airlines announces that Flight 127 to Houston and El Paso is delayed. Continental's Flight 127 to Houston and El Paso is now scheduled to depart at 3:00 from Gate 7. Passengers on Continental 127 are advised that their flight will depart from Gate 7 at 3:00.

4. Peoplexpress announces that Flight 881 to New York City's La Guardia Airport at 2:55 will depart from Gate 2 and will start boarding in 10 minutes. At this time will passengers who need special help in boarding please go to Gate 2 for Peoplexpress 881 to New York La Guardia at 2:55.

5. Streamline Air Flight 403 to Atlanta with connections to Miami and other points south will depart on schedule at 3:05 from Gate 4. We repeat: Streamline Air 403 will depart as scheduled at 3:05 for Atlanta. Passengers should make their seat selection at Gate 4 prior to boarding which will begin in 5 minutes.

Unit 13

A. Airport announcements

1. This is the last call for flight 932 for Syracuse, now boarding at Gate 14. Scheduled departure time is 3:25.

2. Flight 217 with nonstop service to Caracas is boarding at Gate 34. The flight is 10 minutes behind schedule and will depart at 3:40.

3. Flight 558 with service to Hartford, Connecticut and Springfield, Massachusetts is now ready for boarding at Gate 26. The flight will depart on schedule at 3:45.

4. Pan Am's flight 563 to Detroit is now pre-boarding. Passengers with small children or who require special help in boarding should go now to Gate 12. The flight will leave as scheduled at 4:30.

5. Will Pan Am passenger Rita Chambers holding a ticket on flight 67, scheduled to depart for San Francisco at 4:30, please go to Gate 32 for a new seat assignment prior to boarding. Ms. Rita Chambers.

6. Passengers for Los Angeles, may I please have your attention. Pan Am's nonstop service to Los Angeles, Flight 811 scheduled to depart at 4:30 has been delayed due to late arrival from London. Flight 811 will now depart at 4:50 from Gate 30. Boarding will begin in 15 minutes.

B. In-flight announcements

1. Good afternoon, ladies and gentlemen. This is your captain, Tom Brown. We'd like to welcome you aboard flight 811 and to apologize for the delay. We had some bumpy weather over the Atlantic and arrived late from London. Now we are experiencing another slight delay as we wait for clearance from Air Traffic Control. We don't expect it will be more than five minutes, and we hope to arrive in Los Angeles at about 7:30 local time.

2. This is the captain again. I just wanted to apologize again for the delays and to let you know that we are almost back on schedule. Our Boeing 767 is cruising at an altitude of about 30,000 feet at an airspeed of 560 miles per hour. We are above the state of Maryland and that's Washington, D.C. over to the left of the plane. The temperature in Los Angeles is 79° Fahrenheit (that's 26° Celsius). The day is clear and sunny—really unusual for Los Angeles. We ask that while you are in your seats you keep your seat belts fastened in case we hit some unexpected turbulence.

3. We're beginning our approach now to Los Angeles International Airport. Please make sure your seat belt is securely fastened, return your seat and tray to their original upright position, and extinguish all smoking materials. No smoking is allowed until you are in the airport terminal building.

4. We hope you have had a pleasant and enjoyable flight and we'd like to thank you for flying Pan Am today. Please remain in your seat until the plane has come to a complete and final stop at the gate. If you have any questions about connecting flights, please see the Pan Am agents who will meet our flight.

Unit 15

Bargaining

Sally: Excuse me. How much do you want for this bowl?

Stand Owner: Let's see.... Hmm ... That's an outstanding piece of Depression glass—in perfect shape. It's worth eighty bucks.

Sally: Eighty dollars! Oh, I couldn't possibly pay that much. It's a shame. It really is nice.

Stand Owner: I said it was *worth* eighty bucks. I'm only asking sixty.

Sally: Sixty dollars?

Stand Owner: Yeah, it's a real bargain.

Sally: Oh, I'm sure it is. But I can't afford that.

Stand Owner: Well, look. Tell you what I'll do. I'll make it fifty-five. I can't go any lower than that.

Sally: I'll give you thirty-five.

Stand Owner: Thirty-five! Come on, lady. You've got to be kidding. I paid more than that for it myself. Take it for fifty. It's worth every penny.

Sally: Well, maybe I could give you forty.

Stand Owner: Forty-eight. That's my final price.

Sally: Forty-five.

Stand Owner: Make it forty-seven.

Sally: O.K. Forty-seven.

Stand Owner: Let me wrap it up for you. There you are, lady—a real bargain!

Sally: Yeah, thanks a lot.